HOW DO YOU KNOW IT'S TRUE?

HOW DO
YOU KNOW
IT'S TRUE?

David Klein
and Marymae E. Klein

CHARLES SCRIBNER'S SONS · NEW YORK

Grateful acknowledgment is made for the use of illustrative material on the following pages: page 18, from *Invitation to Psychology* by John B. Houston *et al.* (Academic Press); page 81, the National Academy of Sciences; pages 128-129, the National Center for Health Statistics. Pages 48, 116, 148-149 copyright © 1983/1984 by The New York Times Company. Reprinted by permission.

Library of Congress Cataloging in Publication Data
Klein, David, 1919–   How do you know it's true?
    Includes index.
    Summary: Examines, through pertinent examples and anecdotes, how reality is often distorted by commonly held myths and misconceptions, misleading advertising, and misuse of statistics and survey results. Also discusses ways of developing critical thinking.
    1. Truth—Juvenile literature.   2. Reasoning—Juvenile literature.   [1. Truth.   2. Reasoning.   3. Thought and thinking]
I. Klein, Marymae.   II. Title.
BC171.K57   1984   160   84-14023
ISBN 0–684–18225–4

For Ben and Sara
who seem statistically improbable

Contents

1

What—and Whom—Can You Really Believe?

For every time she shouted, "Fire,"
They only answered "Little Liar!"
And therefore when her Aunt returned
Matilda, and the House, were burned.
          —Hilaire Belloc

As far back as you can remember, all sorts of people have been telling you all sorts of things. First your parents and your friends, then teachers, textbook writers, newspaper editors, television personalities, and advertisers, have been showering you with advice, ideas, and "facts."

When you were younger, you probably believed that everything you were told was true—even the existence of Santa Claus or the visits of the tooth fairy. But now, as you become more mature and more sophisticated, you've begun to question the truth of some of the messages you receive. Indeed, you're becoming aware that some of the "facts" people tell you are flatly contradicted by other "facts" that you hear from other people or come across in the course of your reading.

Your mother, for example, may scold you for eating "junk foods," but *Consumer Reports,* after analyzing a sample of Big Macs and other fast-food fare, concludes that some of the so-called junk foods are actually quite nutritious (although peanut-butter sandwiches are a good deal cheaper). A teacher may tell you that college graduates earn more money than high-school graduates, but your best friend is convinced that construction workers and hairdressers earn more than teachers and librarians—without wasting four years at college. A newspaper article tells you that the earlier you marry, the more likely you are to get divorced; yet your own parents, who may have married as soon as they finished high school, seem quite happy and have never considered divorce.

How do you decide which of these contradictory ideas to accept? How do you sort out the sense from the nonsense in the dozens of messages you receive every day? How can you make sure that you yourself are not talking nonsense to other people? That is what this book is all about.

We think you'll find that learning to distinguish between what is true and what is half true or downright false is both interesting and satisfying, but we would be dishonest if we were to promise you that it will always be easy. It would be easy, of course, if we could furnish you with some magic formulas that worked every time. But there are no such formulas. In fact, you'll discover that for some very important questions there are no "right" or "wrong" answers.

It would be easy, too, if we could tell you how to sort everyone you meet into one of two classes: stupid, dishonest "bad guys" who always tell lies, and intelligent, honest "good guys" whose statements can always be trusted. But the problem is not that simple. Even people who may have much to gain by misleading you—salesmen, politicians, advertisers— tell the truth much of the time. And most of the people who have your interests very much at heart—parents, friends, and teachers—talk nonsense some of the time. And so, judging the truth of a statement by the motives of the person making it is just as unreliable as deciding that anyone who looks you straight in the eye and speaks without hesitation or stammering is telling you the truth.

WHY PEOPLE TALK NONSENSE

There are several reasons why most people—yourself included—talk nonsense at least some of the time. In fact, as you read the next few pages, you may find that we label as nonsense some ideas that you have not only accepted but have passed on to other people. But there's no reason to feel embarrassed; nobody can be right all the time. If, however, you can understand what it is that makes some statements nonsensical, you are likely to make fewer of them in the future.

Many people simply accept and repeat what they're told. Because none of us can possibly check the accuracy of every statement we hear or read, we tend to accept a good deal of information on faith—especially if it comes from a source who "ought to know." For example, you may believe, along with many other people, that a course in driver education makes students safer drivers than they would be without one. After all, if it didn't, why would your school offer the course, and why would insurance companies offer discounts to students who have passed the course, and why would some states allow them to apply for a driver's license a year earlier?

Yet social scientists who have systematically studied the accident records of thousands of students all over the country conclude that a driver-education course does *not* cause students to have fewer accidents than students who were taught to drive by parents or friends. If your driver-education teacher promises you that the course will make you a safer driver, he's dead wrong, even though he is probably not misleading you deliberately. He just hasn't bothered to read the research reports.

Are the insurance companies wrong in giving driver-educated teenagers a discount, and are some states wrong in licensing them a year earlier? Not entirely, but these are questions to which we'll return in Chapter 5.

Many people base their "knowledge" on proverbs and other folk wisdom. Because some proverbs have been around for centuries and because they're widely known, many people think they express some sort of eternal wisdom. But it's easy to find a pair of proverbs that contradict each other, even though each sounds sensible enough by itself. Do "fools rush in where angels fear to tread," or is it true that "he who hesitates is lost"? Do "birds of a feather flock together" or do "opposites attract each other"?

Proverbs, in fact, are so plentiful that it's easy to find one that supports what you *want* to believe rather than what is necessarily true. The saying that "absence makes the heart grow fonder," however, is clearly contradicted by the rising divorce rate among couples whose jobs require them to live apart and who see each other only on weekends.

Many people base their "knowledge" on common sense. The trouble with statements based on common sense is that they may be perfectly *logical* but nevertheless quite wrong. Suppose, for example, someone asked you to predict whether college attendance would go up or down during times of recession and high unemployment. Your common sense might lead you to predict that attendance would drop—because going to college costs money and many people have less money during a recession. But you might just as logically predict that attendance would go up—because young people who can't find jobs decide to go to college to use their time productively and to improve their job skills.

How can we know which prediction is the right one? By actually measuring college enrollments during times of prosperity and recession. When we do this, we find that during recessions attendance generally goes up, not down.

We are not saying that common sense *always* leads to the wrong conclusions. But, as we shall see in Chapter 5, it can be trusted only when it's used in connection with solid evidence.

Many people place too much faith in "experts." If you want trustworthy answers to complex questions, your best bet is to read something written by an expert in the field. Experts don't know all the answers, and they are not always right, but they are more likely to be right than people who know less about the subject than they do.

The problem is that experts in one area of knowledge are often assumed to be experts in other areas. And the experts themselves, because they are so respectfully consulted about problems on which they are *not* experts, sometimes come to believe that they really are very wise and that their opinions on any subject should be taken seriously.

So, for example, the Nobel-prize–winning physicist William Shockley has for years been arguing in public that blacks are less intelligent than whites. Many unsophisticated people, who seem to believe that "anyone who wins a Nobel prize must be brilliant," don't stop to ask themselves why a physicist, no matter how brilliant, should necessarily be an authority on a question that involves psychology, genetics, anthropology, and sociology. But the fact is that very few, if any, geneticists, psychologists, anthropologists, and sociologists agree with Dr. Shockley.

Many people believe that "seeing is believing." If you've "seen it with your own eyes," it's tempting to believe that what you've seen must be true. But *seeing* is not always a reliable process, because what you see depends on where you are standing. If you rely on your own eyes, you would have to believe that the earth is flat—unless you were an astronaut. They are the only people who have *seen* that the earth is a sphere, although navigators and astronomers proved that it was spherical many centuries before anyone *saw* that it was.

No matter how sharp our vision, none of us can see very far; what we see is what goes on around us. This is why people who have lived all their lives in large cities can't really understand what life on a farm is like—and why farmers have some peculiar ideas about life in the big city.

Seeing has other limitations. We tend to see not what is really there but what we expect to see, and for this reason we often misinterpret our observations. If, as you drive through a slum area, you see a group of men standing on a street corner in the middle of the day, are you seeing "a bunch of loafers hanging around instead of looking for a job" or a construction crew waiting for the truck that will pick them up and take them to work?

Many people draw conclusions from faulty evidence. Some people from small towns are afraid to visit New York or any other large city because "hundreds of murders and muggings happen there every year." What they overlook is that these cities contain millions of people and that the murder rate *per 1,000 people* is a lot lower in New York than in such smaller cities as El Paso, Texas, or Columbia, South Carolina.

Similarly, because airplane crashes almost always make newspaper headlines but automobile crashes rarely do, many people feel safer driving across the country than flying by commercial airline. Yet they are more than five times more likely to be killed in their car than in a DC-10 or a 747.

Many people draw faulty conclusions from good evidence. A few years ago, when the highway speed limit was reduced to fifty-five miles per hour in an attempt to conserve gasoline, the number of people killed in automobile accidents dropped sharply. Can you conclude from this—as many newspaper editors and police officials have concluded—that high speed is the major cause of fatal accidents? Not if you know that during this same period people did considerably less driving in an attempt to save gasoline—and if you are not on the road, your chances of being killed in an automobile accident become very low indeed. We may suspect that the lowering of the speed limit *may have contributed* to the drop in fatalities, but this is quite different from concluding that high speeds "cause" highway deaths.

Actually, after the fifty-five-mile speed limit had been in effect for a couple of years, the number of people killed in accidents began rising to its earlier level. Did this occur because people began disregarding the speed limit, or because they became accustomed to the higher price of gasoline and began driving more, or because they were driving smaller cars, which give their occupants less protection? Or were all three factors involved? Nobody knows for sure.

Many people believe whatever makes them comfortable. People who tell you that "you always get what you pay for" often get poor value for their money because, as you may have discovered for yourself, we *don't* always get what we pay for, and price is not a completely reliable guide to quality. But learning how to judge the quality of what you buy and then shopping around for the best value does take time and effort, and some people find it easier simply to choose the highest-priced version of whatever it is they're shopping for and to justify their expenditure with a common but untrue statement.

Many people see the world as they would like it to be rather than as it really is. People who say that "any American child can grow up to be president of the United States" like to believe that our country offers everyone an equal opportu-

nity for success and distinction. But they disregard the fact
that no child of poor parents has ever become president.
(Abraham Lincoln's parents, despite what you may have
learned in your history class, were *not* poor—that is, they
were no worse off than most of their fellow citizens.) And
today running for the presidency requires more education
and more money than a child of poor parents is likely to
acquire.

Women and blacks are also exceptions to the "anybody can
become president" notion. A woman or a black *may* become
president some day but, despite the efforts of Jesse Jackson,
Walter Mondale, and the feminist movement, most political
scientists think that that day is a long way off.

The belief that "every student has the opportunity to go to
college" also reflects wishful thinking rather than reality.
Statistics show that if you stand in the top fifth of your class
and your parents are college educated and well-to-do, you are
more than twice as likely to get a college education as a class-
mate with the same academic standing whose parents are
factory workers with only a high-school education.

Many people think in terms of "all or nothing." When they
hear a "fact" about a certain group, some people automatically apply that fact to every member of the group. It is a
fact, for example, that teenaged drivers as a group have many
more fatal automobile accidents than adult drivers, but it is
also a fact that the vast majority of teenaged drivers have no
serious accidents at all. It is true that adolescence is a time
when children are likely to rebel against their parents, but it
is also true that most adolescents get along with their parents
rather well.

Many people base their beliefs on personal experience. If
you know some older people who started out in life poor but

eventually became well-to-do by dint of hard work and persistence, you may have heard them say—often and at tedious length—that hard work is the sure path to success and that today's poor people "ought to get out and hustle, just as I did, instead of loafing around on welfare." What these people fail to recognize is that their success came at a time when the whole American economy was growing much more rapidly than it is today and that the kind of job that gave them their start was far more plentiful and required less education. Scientific studies show that most people on welfare would be very eager to work if only they could find a job, but describing them as lazy and idle makes these older people feel rather virtuous by comparison.

WILL KNOWING THE TRUTH MAKE YOU POPULAR, RICH, AND HAPPY?

By this point in your reading, you have probably reached a correct, if disappointing, conclusion: it's just not possible to classify people into one of two groups: people who talk sense and people who talk nonsense. The fact is that all people— you, your friends and classmates, your parents, your teachers, the people who write newspaper articles and television programs—are likely to be wrong about some things, not because they are stupid or devious but for all of the perfectly human reasons we've suggested in this chapter.

You may also have reached a second conclusion—also correct: learning to distinguish sense from nonsense is not a simple matter. And even when you've finished this book you won't always be able to tell whether a statement is true or not. What you *will* be able to do—at least much of the time —is to suspect or detect statements that are *probably* false.

And you will learn, also, that in many situations answering a question with "I don't know" marks you not as an ignorant person but as an intelligent and thoughtful one.

The question you need to ask yourself now is whether reading the rest of this book is worth your time and effort. We think it is—for two reasons.

To begin with, learning to detect and reject wrong or misleading information will help you avoid making bad decisions —trivial ones, such as buying a shoddy stereo set because you were fooled by a slick advertisement for it, or major ones, such as choosing the wrong college, the wrong career, or the wrong spouse.

But the second reason may be far more important. Although thus far we have emphasized the information you have been *receiving*, you will, for the rest of your life, be giving advice and communicating ideas to other people—to your family, your friends, your teachers, and, later on, to your boss, your fellow workers, your spouse, and your children. Since most of what you tell them will be based on what you think are the "facts," you are almost certain to tell them a lot of nonsense unless you have learned to discriminate between sense and nonsense yourself.

Talk a lot of nonsense and your listeners, if they believe you, may make bad decisions. Talk a lot of nonsense and you are not likely to win many arguments or convince people about anything much. Talk a lot of nonsense and you won't be taken seriously by people whose respect you really want —your college professors, people whom you'd like to have as friends, people with whom you'd like to work.

On the other hand, once you've learned to detect obvious nonsense—and to be skeptical about statements that you used to accept uncritically—are you likely to be any happier? This is a hard question to answer. True, these skills can make you the star of the debating team and can win you the respect of educated people, but they can also cause you some difficulties and discomfort.

Challenging the "facts" that your friends, your parents, or your teachers accept without question is hardly the best way to achieve popularity. Throughout history people have been shunned, punished—even put to death—for questioning the truth of "what everybody knows." And, since most untrue ideas persist because they are comforting, challenging them is not likely to make you feel more comfortable. After all, wouldn't you feel better believing that "money can't buy happiness" or that "anybody who wants to can go to college," even though neither of these statements is true?

Since we can't promise you popularity or personal comfort if you learn what this book can teach you, why should you make the effort to continue reading it? When the English philosopher John Stuart Mill was faced with a similar question, his answer was, "It is better to be Socrates dissatisfied than a pig satisfied."

What's your answer?

2

How We Know What We Know— and Why We're So Often Wrong

He thought he saw a Banker's Clerk
Descending from the 'bus:
He looked again, and found it was
A Hippopotamus:
　　　　　—Lewis Carroll

As we've noted, much of the information we receive is likely, for various reasons, to be wrong. And if we accept such wrong information at face value, we can mislead both ourselves and others. Often, however, the information that is offered us—in books, or television programs, or conversations—may be correct, but we distort or misinterpret it for reasons that lie within each of us. And so, before examining how and why people *transmit* wrong information—as we'll do in the next chapter—we need to understand the reasons why all of us *receive* information incorrectly even when that information is true.

TRUE OR FALSE?

You can make a start at this by trying to mark each of the following statements true or false:

1. Water boils at 212° F., or 100° C.
2. Your nine-o'clock English class will meet tomorrow as scheduled.

3. If you drop your cat out of a sixteenth-floor window, she'll be killed.

The chances are pretty good that you marked all three statements as true, even though, strictly speaking, each of them may be false some of the time. Water, for example, boils at a lower temperature at high altitudes. (This is why it takes longer to hard-boil an egg in Denver than in New York.) As for tomorrow's English class, there is always a possibility (even though it's only one in several million) that all thirty students and the teacher will be stricken with a bad cold and not show up. And a very few cats *have* survived falls out of tall buildings. (According to the ASPCA, the current record, actually, is forty-two floors.)

But for all practical purposes, most of the time, the three statements are true *enough* for you to base your behavior on them. You're not likely to plunge your hand into boiling water (even in Denver)—or to cut your English class in the belief that nobody else will show up—or to throw the cat out of a sixteenth-floor window to see what will happen to her. In all these cases you "know better."

In fact, even though you may have lived only about one-fifth of your full life expectancy, you "know" an incredible amount of information that is "true" enough to enable you to live your life fairly smoothly. And you have learned this information in a variety of ways. You learned the boiling point of water, for example, from *a trustworthy authority*—a textbook or a science teacher. You predicted the meeting of your English class on the basis of considerable *personal experience* with teachers and with classes. And your *common sense*, applied to what you know about cats and about the law of gravitation, allowed you to predict the fate of the falling cat. In short, through many years of learning facts and applying common sense to them, you are able to make a great many generalizations and predictions that turn out to be correct.

SOME HARDER QUESTIONS

But now let's try the following true-or-false test:

1. The senior executives of a corporation are more likely to have heart attacks than the unskilled workers.
2. Poor people are more likely than well-to-do people to buy the cheaper, "no-frills" canned goods rather than the more expensive, nationally advertised brands.
3. Lawyers who make dramatic courtroom appearances earn more money than those who spend most of their time in their law offices.

If you answered "True" to Statement 1, you have lots of company; most people do. But it's not especially good company, because the statement is, in fact, false. Research has shown that unskilled workers are three or four times more likely than senior executives to suffer heart attacks.

Why, then, do so many people mark it true? Most of them say that their answer was "just a matter of common sense": senior executives have heavier responsibilities (true) and they work longer hours (also true); therefore they suffer more stress, which, combined with the fact that their work is sedentary, leads to more heart attacks.

But one could argue *just as logically* that the unskilled worker is more fearful of losing his job (true), that he is often worried about making ends meet (true), that he enjoys his work far less than the executive (true), and that all these sources of stress, combined with the fact that he is less likely to get good medical care (true), make him more vulnerable to heart attacks than the president and vice-presidents of his company.

Common sense by itself, then, can't give us the correct answer. But since common sense could have led to *either* answer, why do most people mark the statement as true? One reason is that most of us spend more time thinking and reading about executives than about unskilled workers. Most young people, for example, would rather become executives than unskilled workers, and consequently they pay more attention to executive than to blue-collar life-style. And when an executive dies of a heart attack, his death is likely to be reported in the media, whereas thousands of unskilled workers die every day without any public notice. Thus, most of us, *as a result of our experience and interests,* have developed a "mind set" that predisposes us to one point of view rather than another and makes it hard for us to perceive reality objectively.

This mind set influences the way in which we interpret almost everything we see. Try, for example, without reading any further, to enter the correct numbers at either end of the following series:

_____ 34 42 72 96 _____

Unless you live in New York City, you probably spent several very frustrating minutes trying to work out a mathematical relationship among the numbers—*because this is the kind of problem you've encountered many times on intelligence tests or on the Scholastic Aptitude Test.* But if you're a New Yorker, you might possibly have recognized these numbers as the express stops on the Broadway subway line—and you would have filled in the blanks as 14th Street and 125th Street, respectively. (Even most young New Yorkers, however, have the same mind set as you did on this problem.)

Mind set also influenced your answer to Statement 2—especially if you marked it "True" (which, once again, is wrong). If your family is not poor (and the chances are better than eight to one that it isn't, because poor people have few opportunities to come across books like this one), your family discussions about budgeting and your own experiences at the supermarket have probably taught you a good deal about shopping for "best buys," and you're likely to have learned—perhaps from *Consumer Reports*—that at least some of the "no-frills" brands offer better value than the heavily advertised national brands.

If you applied your common sense to your own experience, you would naturally conclude that poor people, who have to stretch their money further, would be even more eager to avoid the costlier items. But what you may not have taken into account—if you have not lived among or even known any poor people—is that the poor (1) are less likely to be informed about no-frills brands, (2) are less likely to shop in supermarkets that carry these brands, and (3) generally do not read *Consumer Reports* and therefore feel more secure with familiar, widely advertised brands than with those that are unknown and unadvertised. At least, these are the findings of several researchers who have systematically studied the shopping behavior of poor people and conclude, as the title of one of their books puts it, that *The Poor Pay More*.

Your mind set—this time shaped by the media rather than by your family—may have caused you to answer "True" to Statement 3, about lawyers. (Once again, it's false!) Most people answer it wrong simply because very few of us actually see real lawyers at work. Instead, we get our impressions from television, newspapers, and perhaps a book or two written by a prominent criminal lawyer. Because the kind of law practiced outside the courtroom is almost always hard for us to understand (and therefore boring), both newspapers and television programs, in striving to be constantly interesting, tend to show us dramatic, easy-to-understand criminal trials. This is why we get the impression that any truly successful lawyer spends most of his time haranguing a jury. In real life, there are only a few prominent and very successful criminal lawyers, because most defendants in criminal cases can't afford legal fees—a fact that television dramas conveniently overlook. Most successful and widely respected lawyers pride themselves on their ability to settle disputes without having to appear in court.

If you "failed" this true-false test, don't feel depressed. It was not set up to prove that you're stupid. (Actually, more than 90 percent of reasonably bright college students fail all three questions.) Rather, it was intended to demonstrate that most people who try to apply common sense to questions with which they're not familiar are likely to come up with the wrong answers because their mind sets cause them to select certain facts and points of view and to overlook others that may be just as relevant.

MIND SETS—YOURS AND OTHERS

Thus far, we've used *mind set* as a very general term to describe our tendency to see only one side of an issue or to misinterpret what we see "with our own eyes." But if we are to become sufficiently aware of it so that we can make objective judgments, we need to look more closely at the forces that shape it.

To some extent each of us has a mind set that is completely individual, because at any one time it is the product of our sex, our age, our upbringing, our past experiences, our immediate situation, our mood, and dozens of other factors.

Since no two of us are identical, no two mind sets can be identical. In fact, the differences between your mind set and anyone else's can be revealed to some extent by a psychological device known as the Thematic Apperception Test. This test, which consists of a series of ambiguous pictures, requires you to "tell the story" that each picture illustrates. As you might expect, no two people tell the same story, because no two mind sets are identical.

Yet it is obvious, too, that to a large extent our mind sets must be similar, because if we did not agree about the meaning of what we see, we could not communicate with one another meaningfully—or, in fact, live together in any sort of harmony. And so it is true that, unless we are mentally ill or

Tell the story that you think this picture illustrates. Then ask two or three of your friends to do the same. You'll find that no two stories are alike—and none of them, of course, is "correct."

retarded, we do, as human beings and as Americans, have large areas of our mind set in common—but even this shared mind set can lead us occasionally to reject or misinterpret reality. Let's look at some examples.

A Matter of Mood

How you feel at any given moment can influence your interpretation of "reality" rather dramatically. Have you ever, during a sleepless night, been absolutely certain that the creaking of your house, as the heating system cooled down, was the stealthy tread of a burglar or a murderer? And did you feel a bit silly about your fears the next morning? On the other hand, have you ever felt that you had a "great" teacher in a class that you almost failed—or a "lousy" one in a class in which you were the top student? And did you perhaps change your mind about both a year or two later?

A Matter of Experience

Every one of us, no matter how broad our education or our reading or our travel, can have only limited experience. And so, like the blind men examining the elephant, we're likely to reach wrong conclusions if we generalize on the basis of our personal experience or if, for lack of experience, we uncritically accept whatever we hear or read.

Many farmers and their children, for example, dread visiting the "big, bad city" because they are convinced that they will be mugged or cheated. And many city dwellers, with no better justification, think that people who live in small towns are "a bunch of dumb hicks who spend their time sitting around the general-store cracker barrel."

To some extent television, magazines, movies, and other media have not only made faraway places more familiar to us but have also made different parts of the country more alike. But the fact that Brunswick, Georgia, with its Sears store, its Toyota dealership, and its McDonald's, is much more similar to Brunswick, Maine, than it was fifty years ago makes it even easier for us to assume that we "know all about" a community or a group of people with whom we've had no experience whatever.

The limitations on our experience are especially dangerous when we try to understand people who are different from us in education, or income, or ethnic background. Because most of us live in neighborhoods in which our neighbors are very much like ourselves, we have very little daily, face-to-face experience with people who are richer or poorer, better- or worse-educated, or different from us in skin color. Without such direct experience, it is all too easy for us to assume either that such people are "just like us" or that "they're completely different"—neither of which is accurate.

At your own high school, for example, perhaps 92 percent of your classmates plan on going to college and 10 percent intend to study medicine or law. Can you assume that their plans are typical of high-school students all over the country? Not if you know that in some communities only 30 percent of high-school graduates go on to college and that many of the most ambitious ones plan to be truck drivers or hairdressers. On the other hand, you'd be quite wrong in assuming that in those communities most high-school students are "just not interested" in going to college or are "too dumb" to get in.

A Matter of Knowledge

Just as our experience is limited, so, too, is our knowledge. And so, very often, we make judgments without knowing enough about the issue we are judging. Suppose, for example, that the motorcyclists in your state are petitioning the state legislature to repeal the compulsory-helmet law, which most states have adopted because research has shown that helmets save lives and reduce injuries in accidents.

Would you agree with the motorcyclists' argument that "if we want to kill ourselves, it's nobody's business but our own"? Or would you strongly disagree if you were aware that (1) the medical and funeral bills of many motorcycle-accident victims are paid by the taxpayers, (2) motorcycle deaths increase the insurance premiums that all of us pay, and (3) many motorcycle-accident victims leave behind them spouses and children who must then be supported by all taxpayers through welfare payments? Many people who support one side of an issue would probably change sides if they knew all the facts.

Good Guys and Bad Guys

We all have a tendency to classify people either as "good guys" (who can do no wrong) or "bad guys" (who presumably can do no right). There are two flaws in this kind of oversimple classification. The first, known as the *halo effect,* is that it prevents you from seeing people as they really are— from recognizing, for example, that your best friend may have a streak of selfishness or that the teacher you hate most may have a passionate interest in his subject and a genuine concern for his students.

The second flaw can be illustrated by the Navaho saying, "Do not speak ill of any man until you have walked a mile in his moccasins." Most of the people we classify as "bad" are simply pursuing goals that we disagree with. If, for example, you are strongly concerned with the state of the environment, you are likely to regard the oil companies that want to explore for oil offshore or on public lands as "bad guys." Yet these companies cannot be accurately labeled as villainous. They simply disagree with your view that a healthful environment is preferable to the profits and employment that they anticipate from more oil drilling and production. If you were the vice-president of an oil company, what would your position be?

This is not to suggest that you should abandon your defense of a clean and safe environment simply because you "understand" the position taken by your opponents. Rather, understanding their point of view can help you fight them more effectively than you can if you simply see them as "bad guys."

When You're Part of the Action

If you've ever waited impatiently for a westbound bus, you probably noticed that all the buses seemed to be eastbound that day. After three eastbound buses passed you, you may even have begun to suspect that all the eastbound buses were returning westbound by some secret, invisible route only to come eastbound again before your eyes.

Of course, once you considered your suspicion, you probably felt a bit foolish, because you realized that every eastbound bus had to be westbound half the time. But stop and think a moment. *Did you actually see more eastbound than westbound buses?* Of course you did: given your situation, you could see no westbound buses pass you, because you boarded the first one that came along. Had you been an objective observer standing at the bus stop with a tally board counting east- and westbound buses, you would have come up with an even count for each direction. But because you were an impatient passenger, very directly involved, you could not possibly have observed the total flow.

Whenever you are personally involved in an issue, you are

likely to find it almost impossible to be detached and objective. If, for example, you are both overweight and unhappy about it, you are likely to believe the diet-pill advertisements far more willingly than the conclusions of nutritionists (who say unanimously that the only reliable way to lose weight is to cut down on your food intake).

Even well-trained scientists risk losing their objectivity when they are personally involved in experiments intended to test a theory that they cherish. To avoid this risk, they take a number of precautions that we'll discuss in Chapter 5.

Sour Grapes and Sweet Lemons
Another tendency we all share is an inability to deal simultaneously with two ideas that are inconsistent with each other. In such situations, we tend to distort one of the ideas so as to reduce the inconsistency and thus make ourselves feel more comfortable.

Perhaps you've experienced this distortion after you tried to get a date with someone and your best efforts failed. Before trying for the date, you had two ideas that were perfectly consistent:

1. The person you were about to ask was a desirable date.
2. You are an acceptable dating partner.

After your rejection, however, these two ideas were contradictory, because *if* the other person were really desirable and *if* you were in fact acceptable, a date would have resulted. How, then, did you resolve the contradiction? Did you change your mind about your own acceptability? Or did you decide, as most people in your situation do, that your intended date, who was very attractive to you before the rejection, "was really not all that great after all"? And was either of your conclusions necessarily true?

This phenomenon—which psychologists call *cognitive dissonance reduction* but which Aesop recognized almost 2,500 years ago in his fable about the fox who, unable to snatch a bunch of attractive grapes, decided that they were sour—often affects issues far more important than dating. Suppose that, 200 years ago, you held these two ideas:

1. The Bible tells you to do unto others what you would have others do unto you.
2. It is perfectly acceptable to keep blacks in slavery, often under inhuman conditions.

How would you have reduced your cognitive dissonance? You might, of course, have rejected the Bible, but this would have been unthinkable if you were a God-fearing Christian. The alternative was much more comfortable: blacks don't count as "others," because they're not really human. In fact, it's the duty of good Christians to "take care of them" because they're not capable of taking care of themselves. This kind of "reasoning" accounts in large part for the discrimination against blacks that has continued to our own time.

A Matter of Stereotypes

Another reason why we often have trouble in perceiving "what's really there" is that, in thinking about any group of people, we all tend to use what social scientists call a *stereotype*—that is, a highly simplified mental picture of what members of that group are like. Thus, for example, when we hear or see the word "teacher" or "policeman," we tend to conjure up a set of characteristics that apply to *all* teachers or all policemen.

Stereotypes are, of course, essential to us when we meet strangers. If, for example, you have to baby-sit for a three-year-old you've never met before, the only guidance you have in dealing with her comes from your stereotype of "what three-year-olds are like." This stereotype will tell you, for example, that three-year-olds are timid with strangers, that they don't have the table manners or the vocabulary of ten-year-olds, and that, unlike people of your own age, they have to be reminded about going to the toilet. In most baby-sitting situations—and, for that matter, in most other un-familiar situations—your stereotypes will help you cope adequately.

But stereotypes have two limitations that create problems for us. First, because they are oversimplifications, they don't apply to all members of the group and they can't tell us everything about the behavior of any one member. And so, for example, the next three-year-old you encounter may, in fact, feel perfectly at home with strangers, may feed himself very neatly while holding a sophisticated conversation, and may be 100 percent housebroken. Yet the fact that one par-ticular three-year-old surprised you does not make your stereotype useless. It still offers you good guidance for deal-ing with the next three-year-old provided you remain aware that *it doesn't fit every individual* and provided that *you're prepared to abandon it as soon as you discover that it doesn't fit.*

A second, and much more serious, limitation of stereotypes is that many of them are inaccurate—either because they are out of date or because they came about through igno-rance, misinterpretation, or hostility. The now-abandoned stereotype of blacks as having "a natural sense of rhythm" stemmed from the fact that, until recently, music and dance were the only activities in which blacks were allowed to be successful. If your stereotype of the Navaho emphasizes their skills in rug weaving and jewelry making, ask yourself whether they have had many opportunities to demonstrate their skills in other activities. It is only very recently, when women have come into the work force in large numbers, that the stereotype of women as frivolous, emotional, and incapable of any serious business undertaking has begun to disappear.

Hostile stereotypes—about "lazy" blacks or "dumb" Polish-Americans or "sharp-dealing" Jews—often center on minority racial or ethnic groups, but they are applied also to groups whom we may envy or whom we see as "better" than ourselves. The stereotypes of the "absent-minded professor," the "mad" scientist, and the "idle" rich all demonstrate this. And so does the stereotype of the high-school "brain" that depicts him as a ninety-eight-pound weakling with thick-lensed glasses and no social life whatever.

Any hostile stereotypes you have would, of course, disappear if you could be familiar with the people they describe. If you had the opportunity to know them intimately or read scientific studies about them, you'd find that professors are no more absent-minded than the rest of us, that scientists are far less likely to be mad than nonscientists, and that most high-school "brains" are in better physical shape and enjoy more active social lives than students with a C average. But since none of us can be familiar with all groups, and since we all (rightly or wrongly) envy or fear some groups, our only defense against being misled by stereotypes is to examine them very carefully—to use them with caution at all times, and to be especially suspicious if they seem at all hostile.

WHAT TO DO ABOUT MIND SET

By this point you may be wondering how—if everyone is handicapped by mind set—anyone can ever arrive at the truth. The process of discounting mind set is far from simple. In fact, if you decide to become a scientist you'll discover that much of your training in scientific method focuses on it. For the moment, your best approach is to *be aware* of the ways in which your mind set influences both your perception and your interpretation of everything you see and hear, whether or not it is accurate in the first place. Often, however, what you see or hear is inaccurate to begin with—because, like you, the whole of American society has a mind set that distorts reality—as we'll see in the next chapter.

3

Santa Claus and Other Problems

"Do you believe in infant baptism?"
"Believe in it? I've seen it with my own eyes."

The chances are pretty good, we suspect, that you don't believe in Santa Claus. We don't mean the people who dress up in red suits and white beards in department stores or at Christmas parties. They're real enough! But if you don't believe in the existence of a kindly old man who climbs down chimneys once a year, you're probably right. No explorer at the North Pole has ever located his workshop, and no airline pilot has ever reported sighting his sleigh on Christmas Eve.

Yet not so many years ago you probably did believe in him and, although you no longer do, you're likely to teach your own children about him when they are very young. Why, then, does the idea of Santa Claus persist when there is no scientific evidence that he exists? After all, we no longer believe in witches, as educated people did for hundreds of years. The answer is that Santa Claus, like many other persistent myths, serves some very useful purposes.

To begin with, parents can use Santa to personify the joys of Christmas and the spirit of giving—and to transmit to their children the magic and excitement of their own childhood, when gifts appeared "mysteriously." But they can also use Santa as a threat ("Santa won't come if you're not good") if they don't want to threaten their children personally. In addition, parents can blame Santa Claus rather than themselves if a gift disappoints their child. And, of course, parents can use the "letter to Santa" to find out the kinds of gifts that their children really want. As for the children, the notion of a midnight visitor who will arrive with unknown goodies is a lot more exciting than knowing that their own parents will set out around the tree presents that they've hidden in the hall closet for the past week or two. And the department stores love Santa Claus because he helps them sell toys at Christmas.

And so, even though Santa Claus isn't "real," he persists because in various ways he makes a great many people feel good or he prevents them from feeling bad. (Not everybody, of course; he's of no comfort to the children of parents too poor to buy the gifts for which their children asked Santa.) But, since the myth of Santa Claus seems to do more good than harm, it remains a part of our thinking even though we know it isn't true.

SOME POPULAR MYTHS

A myth, then, is a belief or idea that persists because it seems to serve a useful purpose even though its truth can't be proven (or may even be disproven) scientifically. Some of these beliefs may have been true at one time but became untrue as our world changed. Others were never true. Like the notion that the earth is flat, they came about through insufficient knowledge but, unlike that notion, they have persisted because they are comforting. Still others, like the statement that "all men are created equal," were never meant to be taken literally but represent some kind of ideal.

But some of the myths in the world around us are a good deal less innocent than the Santa Claus myth. Although many people continue to believe in them because they are comforting, they can also do a lot of harm. In the next few pages, we'll examine a few of the myths that remain alive and well today. As we do so, you might ask yourself how many of them you believe in, even though you no longer believe in Santa Claus.

The Greatest Nation in the World

The belief that we Americans live in the greatest (or the richest or the most powerful) nation in the world is obviously a comforting one, but deciding whether it is true or not raises a very tricky question: How can we measure "greatness"?

If we measure it in terms of economics—that is, the standard of living enjoyed by most people—there is no question that the United States was "the greatest" for the first two centuries of its history. It had the fastest-growing economy in the world and, although not every immigrant rose from rags to riches, the average income of Americans was higher than in any other country. Because conditions encouraged inventiveness, because the population was growing, and because natural resources were plentiful, our country became the world leader in manufacturing and technology, and this, in turn, encouraged further inventiveness.

But times have changed, and today we are no longer the richest country in the world. In at least three countries— Switzerland, Denmark, and Sweden—the average income is higher than ours. In addition, we have a larger proportion of people living in poverty than any industrial European country. Measured by our standard of living, then, we are no longer "the greatest."

If we measure greatness in terms of the quality of life rather than money, once again we must hesitate to hand ourselves the first prize. In fact, a recent University of Pennsylvania research project, which measured more than forty factors that contribute to the quality of life, ranked the United States *forty-first* among the 107 countries studied. In terms of life expectancy—that is, how many years we can expect to live—several countries, including Australia and the Netherlands, outstrip us. In terms of infant mortality—that is, the percentage of babies who die at birth—fourteen countries, including all of the Scandinavian nations, have a lower mortality rate than ours. Our homicide rate is several times higher than that of any other modern industrial country. And, if the greatness of a country can be measured by the happiness or contentment of its citizens, public opinion polls tell us that in recent years Americans have lost some of their former optimism and confidence. More and more of them think that their standard of living will be worse (or no better) than it was in earlier years, and more of them express a wish that they were living in some country other than the United States.

Although none of these facts *proves* that the United States is not the greatest country in the world, or should necessarily lessen our attachment to it, they should certainly give us pause. But since believing that we are the greatest, whether in fact we are or not, makes us feel good, what's the harm in it? Actually, this belief, which social scientists call *ethnocentrism*, can create several problems.

To begin with, it can lead us to take a condescending attitude toward all other countries and their people and to assume that "those foreigners" can't possibly do anything as well as we can. (This, of course, was the assumption made by American automobile manufacturers—until some of them were almost ruined by their Japanese competitors.)

In addition, ethnocentrism encourages us to make comparisons that are favorable to ourselves but that overlook some important details. When a political candidate proudly tells us that the British must work two years to earn enough to buy a small car, while the average American need work less than six months, does he also mention that in Britain higher education and medical care are free? If your parents could be sure that your education and your medical care would cost them nothing, might they feel that two years of earnings was a reasonable price for an automobile? And might free medical care for everyone and free university education for all who qualify make our own country a better place in which to live?

Lastly, if we are convinced that we live in "the greatest nation in the world," we are likely to be contented with our lot, feeling that we have no right to complain, because people in other countries "are a lot worse off." This kind of resignation can close our minds to ideas and alternatives (some of them perhaps imported from other countries) that could make life better for all of us.

The Survival of the Fittest

Many Americans believe that people who are well-to-do have reached their position through intelligence, ambition, hard work, self-discipline, and other admirable characteristics, and that people who are poor deserve their poverty because they are lazy, stupid, unambitious, irresponsible, and generally "inferior."

It is easy enough to see how this belief comforts the well-to-do. For one thing, it removes any guilt they might feel about indulging themselves in luxuries because, according to this notion, such luxuries are the just rewards for their natural superiority and their "good" behavior. In addition, it relieves them of any responsibility for helping the poor because, they are convinced, the poor are too inferior to benefit from any kind of help.

It may be a bit harder to see how this theory comforts the poor—but it does, at least to some extent. If you are poor, and you are convinced that you are "not much good," you may resign yourself to poor schooling and poor jobs because you feel that you can't do any better. On the other hand, if you feel that you are "just as good as anybody else" and you *still* experience bad schooling and few job opportunities, your frustration may become so unbearable that hopelessness and resignation—or violence—may be more acceptable alternatives.

Is there any scientific evidence to support this notion? Although a few scientists still argue that there are differences in intelligence between racial groups, and although most scientists agree that intelligence is to some extent inherited, the overwhelming majority of psychologists and sociologists believe that an individual's abilities and personality are determined less by his genetic inheritance than by the environment in which he is brought up—and that an environment of poverty will produce "inferiority" in the same way in which an environment of affluence produces "superiority."

These scientists have found, for example, that the children of poor mothers are two to four times more likely to die before adulthood than the children of well-to-do mothers, and they conclude that the reason is poor medical care and pregnancy at too early an age, not genetic inferiority.

These scientists agree that the children of the poor score lower on IQ tests, but they point out that poor children don't learn at home the vocabulary or the motivation needed for a high test score. They agree that the children of the poor very often end up on welfare or in low-paying, dead-end jobs, but they blame this not on laziness or stupidity but on the fact that schools in poor neighborhoods don't prepare their students for good jobs or for entrance to college.

To sum up, most scientists are convinced that poor children tend to grow into poor adults not because they are basically inferior but because they are handicapped by growing up in poverty.

The scientific evidence is also rather convincing that the children of the well-to-do are likely to be successful in college and in jobs not because of any inborn qualities but because their parents know how to train them for such success and can afford not only the high cost of a college education but also a variety of experiences (travel, summer camp, private lessons, orthodontia) that may contribute to their children's success.

If two infants—one from poor, uneducated parents, the other from well-to-do and highly educated parents—were accidentally exchanged at birth, would the poor child be likely to grow up successful and the well-to-do child be likely to end up on welfare? More scientists would answer this question with a yes than with a no.

In the face of all this evidence, why is it that so many Americans remain convinced that poor people are "simply no good" and that their poverty is their own fault? One reason is that if we abandoned this view we would feel guilty about the plight of poor people and we would feel obliged to spend tax money to improve their schools, their housing, their nutrition, and other aspects of their lives that now help to keep them in poverty. How much more comfortable for us *not* to increase our taxes by arguing that "it's a waste of money to try to help those lazy, unambitious, irresponsible people." And, of course, if programs for the poor were established that effectively helped them out of poverty, their children would be able to compete on equal terms with the children of the well-to-do for the best jobs our economy has to offer.

From Rags to Riches

Another important myth tells us that any American who is ambitious enough can start life as a poor child and end up as a millionaire. It was this myth, of course, that attracted so many millions of immigrants to "the land of opportunity" during the first two centuries of its existence—and even today it brings us not only thousands of legal immigrants each year but also more thousands who risk their lives to enter the country illegally.

The truth of this myth is hard to determine—especially during our country's early years, when almost no records were kept on people's earnings. But historians generally agree that the vast majority of immigrants arrived poor, lived poor, and died poor. It is true that, because starting up a business in those days required little in the way of education or capital, and because the American economy was growing rapidly, a significant number of people did, in fact, move up from poverty to a decent standard of living, and a very small number did become rich. But this was always the exception, not the rule.

Today, many people are better off financially than their parents or their grandparents, but it is even more difficult to move, in a single lifetime, from rags to riches. Starting a business of one's own is so risky and complicated that more than ninety out of every hundred businesses started each year fail before their first birthday. As for climbing the corporate ladder, many employees of large companies do move to higher positions in the course of their careers, but the distance they move is relatively small, and the height they ultimately reach depends on the height at which they started. It is no longer true that the ambitious young man with a high-school diploma can join a corporation as a mail clerk and wind up as its president. The officers of today's corporations start out with graduate degrees in business or engineering, and very few who reach the top began their careers in "rags."

Why, then, does the "rags to riches" myth persist? Again, because it is comforting to a great many people. If the president of a large corporation can convince himself that "anybody" could have reached his position, he can congratulate himself on his successful competition against all others, and he need not feel guilty about the advantages he may have had as a child of affluent and educated parents. The mail clerk, on the other hand, can relieve the boredom of his job with all sorts of fantasies about becoming an executive, even though he may know that this isn't likely to happen.

We've touched, thus far, on only a few of the many myths that Americans use to make reality more comfortable. Like aspirin tablets, these myths can do much to relieve discomfort from time to time but, again like aspirin, they do nothing to change the basic causes of our discomfort, and, if used too often, can prevent our seeing what our problems really are.

SOME AMERICAN VALUES

Myths are not the only factors in our environment that make reality hard to see. Also involved are our values, or beliefs. Values and beliefs deal with how people *ought to* behave, how life *should be*, but often they conflict with reality—with how people *do* behave or how life actually *is*. Values can be very important as goals and as ethical standards, but they can cause problems when they are confused with reality. Myths can be compared to magic mirrors that make us all look more beautiful than we are. Values are more like mirrors in a carnival fun house: they exaggerate some of our features and make others almost invisible. If we look closely at some of the values that most of us take for granted, we can see how, like myths, they prevent us from seeing the world as it really is.

Tidings of Comfort and Joy
As Americans we tend, more than other people, to "look on the bright side" and take an optimistic view of the future. Most problems, we feel, are likely to be solved if we only persevere and work hard enough (Remember *The Little Engine That Could?*) or if we apply the right technology.

This spirit of optimism has, of course, helped us, both as individuals and as a nation, to overcome all sorts of obstacles and solve all sorts of problems, but it can, if it encourages us to overlook reality, create some very serious problems in the long run. Our optimistic notion that our energy supply was inexhaustible created all sorts of economic troubles, and our optimism about the promise of nuclear power has thus far produced only disappointment and environmental threat. Severe problems about the future availability of water, clean air, and energy sources are not likely to be solved if we simply ignore the realities or optimistically assume that "science will find the answer."

A Sense of Fairness
Both our religious backgrounds ("Blessed are the poor") and our political background ("with liberty and justice for all") have given us a strong sense of fairness—a genuine desire that all people be treated fairly and nobody be unjustly deprived. Although this sense of fairness has had some very important results (laws against discrimination, for example, and pensions for the elderly), it often leads us to think wishfully that life, for many people, is fairer than it actually is.

The saying, "Money can't buy happiness," is a good example of this. It implies that life is fair because the rich, even though they have more money than we do, are not likely to be happy (or at least not as happy as we are). But scientific research finds that life is not as fair as we might like: the rich, according to this research, are happier than the nonrich, and much happier than the poor.

Similarly, we tend to think (again because we'd like life to be fair) that young people who get low grades in academic subjects "are good with their hands." Here, too, research contradicts this belief. Psychologists find that academic skills and manual skills are "positively correlated"—that people who are bright academically are also skilled manually and that those who don't do well in school don't work very well with their hands either.

Yet despite this scientific evidence, these beliefs persist. The headlines in almost every issue of *The National Enquirer* and other supermarket newspapers trumpet the troubles of the rich, and schoolteachers are still convinced that students who don't succeed in academic programs will do well in vocational programs that teach them to work with their hands.

Concern with the Individual

It's likely that all human beings find it easier and more interesting to focus their attention on the behavior of an individual rather than on a mass of statistics that tell us how large numbers of individuals behave, but Americans seem to outdo most other people in this respect. Magazines such as *People*, for example, owe their success entirely to our intense interest in the unusual doings of celebrities of one kind or another.

This concern with the individual rather than the various groups to which he or she may belong has many good consequences. It causes each of us to be regarded as an individual—as Betty Hughes, for example, and not as "a sixteen-year-old girl" or as "a New Yorker" or as "a high-school student" or as "one of the Hughes girls." And being perceived as an individual allows each of us to have our special characteristics recognized, to develop whatever abilities are special to us, and to "do our own thing."

On the other hand, if we focus our attention entirely on the individual, we run the risk of assuming that his or her special behavior or characteristics hold true for the group as a whole. This risk becomes especially serious when individuals are depicted in the news media—because the media are interested only in the *unusual* individual, who is likely not to be typical of the group to which he or she belongs.

When newspapers interview the factory worker who has just won the state lottery prize, for example, it is very easy for other factory workers to think, "The prize could just as well have been won by me." What the newspaper article rarely points out is a fact far more important to its readers: that on that same day 20,000 factory workers bought lottery tickets and won nothing.

A Washington journalist once said of a recent president, "He'd give a hungry kid on the street the shirt off his back and then go back inside the White House and veto a bill providing for school lunches." But this "nearsightedness" is by no means unique. When a local radio station broadcasts a call for blood donations to prolong the life of a child with leukemia, many listeners are likely to respond generously. Yet how many of these people are willing to save about 700 children's lives a year by voting for laws restricting handguns —or even more lives by voting to make seatbelt use compulsory? The immediate, individual situation always exerts a powerful influence on our actions or our thinking—and it often keeps us from seeing the whole picture.

Perhaps a more important consequence of this emphasis on the individual shows up when a person loses his job. Even though most people who get laid off are not themselves at fault but are the victims of periodic recessions, plant closings, technological changes, or other events over which they have no control, our society still seems to feel that unemployment is the individual's "own fault" and that, in one way or another, the unemployed are to blame for their own plight. This same tendency to "blame the victim" often confuses our thinking about failure in school, juvenile delinquency, crime, and other social problems.

WHAT TO DO ABOUT MYTHS AND VALUES

A famous anthropologist once said, "Whoever first identified water, we can be very sure it wasn't a fish." He meant, of course, that a fish is so thoroughly immersed in water that it cannot even imagine such a thing as non-water. The same holds true for many of our values and beliefs. We have been taught them so long and so thoroughly that we tend to take them for granted as "truth" and to defend them against all "heathen" ideas.

None of us can become value-free—and this is fortunate, because a value-free person would not be human. But all of us can become aware that values are not like natural laws. They change over time and they differ not only from one country to another but among different groups in the United States.

One way to see values for what they are is to learn something about the "opposition"—that is, the people who hold somewhat different values. If you come from a home that is solidly Republican, for example, try to talk to some equally solid Democrats or to people who label themselves as Socialists, although these may be harder to find. If you can talk to them seriously, instead of dismissing them as "crazy," you may find that they're no less rational than you are.

Finding people whose values are different from yours may be difficult, because we tend to surround ourselves with people who are very much like us. But reading can be a fine substitute. If your parents subscribe to *U.S. News & World Report* or *Time*, both of which tend to support traditional values, have a look at *Mother Jones*, or *The Nation*, both of which, in very different ways, are "radical." If the paper boy brings only the local paper to your door, have a look, in your town library, at a copy of the *New York Times*. If your social-studies text offers nothing but "the same old stuff," sample a couple of college-level texts in sociology or anthropology.

Above all, feel comfortable in asking the question you asked almost continuously when you were three years old: "Why?" There's nothing juvenile about this question; in fact, scientists ask it constantly. But, as you may remember, it was a youngster rather than an adult scientist who perceived that the emperor was naked.

4

Words, Pictures, and Experts: the Media

"MARINE MARRIED HIS OWN MOTHER"
—*National Enquirer*, February 21, 1984

To many people, the word "media" means television—and possibly that's why they use it, incorrectly, as a singular. But the media include far more than television: a *medium* (singular) is anything that communicates ideas or feelings or opinions or skills to a large number of people. And so, the media include not only television but newspapers, magazines, books (including your school texts), billboard advertisements, museums, radio programs, lectures, plays, concerts, football games, and almost anything else that people see or hear. Some of these are "news media," but all of them are media for mass communication.

Given so broad a definition, you can see that, although you've learned a great deal from your personal experiences and private conversations, most of what you know has come to you through one medium or another. None of us can possibly learn everything we need to know from direct experiences or from chatting privately with our friends. And so your dependence on the media will grow for the rest of your life, along with your increasing need for information. This is why you need to take a critical approach to everything you learn through the media. In doing so, bear in mind that you need to think not only about what you see and hear through the media but also about what you *don't* see and hear because some media (some books, for example) are not available to you or because the available media, for various reasons, choose not to deal with it.

Because the media offer us such a mixed bag, ranging from the comics and Saturday morning television cartoons to scientific journals and the masterpieces of literature, can we say anything useful about their general truthfulness? Aren't some of the messages we get through the media intended to entertain us rather than to teach us anything? And can we take the same critical approach to a comic book and to a textbook on American history? To some extent, we can.

To begin with, the line between entertainment and information isn't easy to draw. Even the Saturday morning television cartoons give their viewers some information. On the other hand, the anchorpersons on television news programs try hard to be entertaining as well as informative. And if you become a physicist, you're likely to get pleasure as well as information from some very-hard-to-read articles in the technical journals written for professional physicists.

But it's when you use the media for sheer entertainment that you are likely to pick up some rather peculiar notions of what the world around you is really like. Psychologists find, for example, that children who choose a steady diet of television cartoons get the impression that most of life's problems can be solved by violence or some other kind of physical activity rather than by thoughtful discussion. (Some children, in fact, become more violent in their own play after watching television cartoon violence, and some find it hard to concentrate on one idea for more than a few seconds, apparently because the cartoons never do.)

Television distorts reality in several ways. For example, people who regularly watch "shoot 'em up" crime shows tend to be more fearful and pessimistic in their daily lives than people who don't. And the young person who decides to become a police officer for the excitement of chasing criminals in cars and shooting at them, "just like the cops on TV," is headed for serious disappointment. In real life more than nine out of ten police officers have never done either and hope very strongly that they never will. (In fact, the police officer who is too enthusiastic about using either gun or gas pedal will usually be dropped from the force.) And in real life, most murderers are not the crazy criminals shown on television but rather ordinary people who kill a friend or a relative unintentionally, usually in the course of a drunken argument.

On the other hand, even the media that you use for information rather than entertainment can give you some very wrong impressions. Your history textbook, for example, may strike you as "full of facts," but some of these "facts" may be either oversimplified or downright questionable. If the book tells you that Columbus "discovered America" in 1492, it omits a lot of information about the earlier Scandinavian and other voyagers and explorers. If it lists the causes of World War II in brisk one-two-three fashion, it oversimplifies issues that historians still argue about. Often, too—for reasons we'll look at shortly—high-school history textbooks omit or downplay or distort incidents that present our country in a less than favorable light.

Of course, with the exception of telephone directories, calendars, supermarket ads, and similar simple, clear-cut media, no medium that presents information to a great many people can be expected to provide "the whole truth and nothing but the truth," because on many issues "the truth" is too complex for many readers or viewers to understand—

or to be presented accurately in a column or two of newsprint or a minute or two on the television screen.

If, for example, your history book were to devote a lot of space to the archaeological evidence for the discovery of America, you would quickly get bored because you would not understand some of it and you would have no time to cover the 300 years of our history in the course of a semester. And so, it's inevitable that if you become a professional historian you will recognize that, on many issues, most high-school history texts are inadequate if not downright wrong.

But since none of us can become an expert on every subject that interests us, we need to recognize that much of what we read or hear is likely to be oversimplified or distorted to some extent. In fact, you can almost be certain that the larger its audience, the more likely is a medium to present a distorted and oversimplified view of the world around us. To see just why and how this occurs, let's have a look at the three "news media," all of which have enormous audiences.

TELEVISION, NEWSPAPERS, AND NEWS MAGAZINES

Has Anyone Bitten Your Dog Lately?
"When a dog bites a man," newspaper editor Joseph Pulitzer advised his reporters, "that's not news. But when a man bites a dog, that's news!" Mr. Pulitzer's advice may have produced "interesting" news stories, but it also explains why television news programs, newspapers, or news magazines often don't tell us what is really going on in the world.

Of course, we all know that in reality we need to worry more (though certainly not much) about being bitten by a dog than about our dog's being bitten by a passing stranger.

But on issues more complex than dog bites, many people forget that an "interesting" news story is interesting precisely because it is *not* what is likely to occur every day to most people.

When newspapers headline a disastrous airplane crash, for example, or a spectacular mass murder, many readers worry more than they should about dying in a plane crash or being murdered. In reality, they are 1,800 times more likely to die of cancer than in a plane crash and 33 times more likely to die of a heart attack than in a homicide. When news programs feature a story on a ten-year-old who was mugged on his way to school, they rarely point out that every day millions of students make the trip to and from school safely. But the very fact that heart-attack victims are far more common than murder victims and safe trips to school are far more common than muggings makes them less "interesting" to the news media—even though you might argue that a news feature or television program on preventing heart attacks might be more useful, and a feature on what ten-year-olds talk about on the way to school might be fascinating.

Problems of Time and Space
In addition to sacrificing realism for "interest," all news media face the problem of filling up a fixed amount of space or time each day—whether or not anything significant has happened. To leave time for commercials, half-hour television news programs can give us only nineteen minutes of news each day; and to allow space for advertisements, newspapers and news magazines can usually print only a certain number of pages no matter what they have to report. For this reason, some very important news events may get too little attention if several of them occur on the same day—or, on the other hand, silly, trivial happenings will get exaggerated

attention on days when nothing much has happened. We always see or read only what the editors and program producers select, but their selection is governed not only by events but also by their limits of space or time.

Given these limitations, the editors of both newspapers and television news programs must make a further decision: How much time or space should we devote to local issues and news (which interest a great many people in our audience) and how much to national and international (which many people find "too dry" but which may have a far greater effect on their lives)? Should we lead off today with a six-car collision on Route 40 or with the latest figures on national unemployment?

You can do a simple experiment to rate your daily newspaper in this respect. For every story on its front page, calculate the distance of the event it describes from your home town. If, for example, you live in Lansing, Michigan, count 0 miles for a Lansing story, 90 miles for a Detroit story, 600 miles for a story from Washington, DC, and 4,000 miles for a story from Ireland. Then add the distances and do the same calculation for a copy of the *New York Times*, the *Los Angeles Times*, or any other big-city newspaper. Try the same experiment with your local television news program and the network news. Depending on where you live, you may discover that the news you're getting is largely limited to your home town or your home state, though in today's world the events most likely to affect your own future don't happen there.

Yet another source of distortion and error that affects both newspapers and television news programs is the time pressure under which reporters work in order to meet a strict deadline —for the morning edition or the seven-o'clock news broadcast. Often this causes inaccuracies or omissions in note taking or picture captioning, some of them trivial but some very serious. Not long ago, for example, newspapers all over the United States published a photograph of a Lebanese baby whose arms had been, according to the caption, blown off during an Israeli bombing raid. We can't know how many of the readers who were outraged by this apparent barbarity read, two days later, that the photograph had been inaccurately captioned and that the baby's amputation had had nothing to do with the bombing. Reputable newspapers usually publish corrections, but it is safe to assume that fewer people read the corrections than the original error.

CORRECTION

An article in Business Day last Wednesday about insurance litigation incorrectly described the status of a $4 billion lawsuit brought by the General Public Utilities Corporation, holding company for the utilities that own the Three Mile Island nuclear plant, against Babcock & Wilcox, builder of the plant. It was settled out of court without determination of fault.

Responsible newspapers such as *The New York Times* publish corrections of errors made in their news stories. But do most of the people who read the stories notice the corrections?

Cutting off the Talking Heads

The limitations we've mentioned thus far are shared by both print media and television, but television, by its very nature, is likely to produce two additional types of distortion. First, recognizing that they are working with a visual medium, television producers are biased toward news stories that can be shown in pictures: fires and explosions, political demonstrations, and other dramatic happenings that give the viewer a feeling of being actually on the scene get preference over "talking heads"—that is, men or women talking to the camera with nothing exciting happening in the background. But some news stories—about inflation, for example, or unemployment—may be analyzed and explained far more thought-fully by a "talking head" than by camera shots of super-market cash registers or lines at the unemployment offices.

When television news coverage is "live," we see only what goes on in front of the television cameras, and this may not be what is really important. But there is an additional problem: people who are aware that they are being filmed by a news crew might behave very differently if the camera were not there. At a student demonstration in Chicago some years ago, the demonstrators were so clearly aware of the presence of television cameras that they set up a chant, "The whole world's watching!" You're right to suspect that some of the behavior of the demonstrators may not have been spontaneous but was put on for the benefit of the television audience. On the other hand, some television crews have been accused, rightly or wrongly, of "rehearsing" the people they interview to make their talk or behavior more "visual" or more "interesting" than it actually is.

Of course, people being interviewed by news reporters can also "put on an act," but the reporter can use her judgment and serve as a filter between the event and the audience, whereas the television journalist doing live coverage has no such control.

Some Words from Our Sponsors

Because no newspaper or television program can exist with-out the support of advertisers or sponsors, it's only natural to wonder whether the big corporations that advertise heavily influence what gets printed or broadcast by threatening to withdraw their support.

This question can't be answered with a clear-cut yes or no. Some newspapers and television programs have resisted such pressures. Newspapers, for example, have refused to fire a movie critic when the movie producer, outraged at a bad review, threatened to withdraw his ads. The CBS television network persisted in showing a controversial documentary on hunting even though almost all its regular sponsors withdrew in the fear of offending their customers who were hunters. In general, though, this kind of independence can be afforded only by newspapers or networks that are so rich that the loss of a few advertisers and sponsors doesn't worry them.

On the other hand, there is good evidence that many of the media yield to pressure, even when the pressure is not exerted on them directly. Many editors simply refuse to publish or broadcast anything that seems likely to offend any advertiser or sponsor. If, for example, your local newspaper runs a column intended to help consumers who have problems, you'll notice that most, if not all, of the cases published in the column deal with small, local merchants, distant mailorder firms, or government agencies and *not* with major corporations or large banks, both of which are heavy advertisers. Government agencies are fair game, of course, because the government does not advertise and because many readers are hostile to "bureaucracy."

Even public television, which relies on grants from corporations such as Mobil and Exxon, is not immune to sponsor pressure. You may have noticed that it does not produce documentaries on the problems of offshore drilling, the profits of oil companies during petroleum shortages, or any other issue that might cast these sponsors in an unfavorable light.

What about Books?
The pressures on book publishers come from several sources. To begin with, many of the largest and most influential publishers are themselves owned by large corporations that have many other interests, and in several instances these corpora-

tions have forced their "captive" publisher to reject or withdraw books that are in some way critical of them or that
present views they oppose.

But probably more important is the fact that, although you
can borrow whatever books you like from your school or
public library, you can choose only from what's available.
And both public library and school library books have recently been subject to increasing censorship—not by librarians (who, as a group, are opposed to censorship) but by
parents and other citizens who arbitrarily decide that some
books—including, for example, *To Kill a Mockingbird*,
Catcher in the Rye, and *Huckleberry Finn*—are not suitable
reading matter for their children.

Obviously, no library can buy every one of the several
thousand books published each year, and some books are
clearly not good enough or important enough to deserve a
place on a library's shelves. The problem of selection is un-
avoidable, and librarians are involved in it almost every day.
But when parents and other citizens decide to override the
librarian's professional judgment, the unprofessional standards they use may deprive you of some very useful and
exciting reading and learning.

Because this censorship of library books does not occur
everywhere, it may not affect you. But censorship of textbooks does, no matter where you live. Not only do you have
no say whatever in the choice of textbooks, but even your
teacher may choose only from a list of texts approved by your
state board. And some state boards, either on their own
initiative or under pressure from extremist citizen groups, set
up standards for content that every textbook must meet if it is
to be approved. To meet the standards in some states, biology
texts, for example, must devote as much space to creationism
(which scientists almost universally reject) as to Darwin's

theory of evolution; in history texts, nothing critical may be said about any of the Founding Fathers—not even the fact that Thomas Jefferson was a slave owner. And the anthologies used in English courses may not contain anything negative about life in the United States.

The fact that you don't live in one of these states offers you no protection. Because these states buy huge numbers of textbooks, publishers are eager to meet their censorship requirements. To avoid the cost of issuing special editions, many publishers incorporate the most severe state restrictions in a single edition that they market nationally—the one you may be using no matter where you live.

ACCORDING TO EXPERT OPINION

As we'll see in the next chapter, most issues on which we must make a judgment or reach a decision—even those that look quite simple—are actually quite complex. This is why many of them cannot be decided without the help of experts. Experts are used not only in court trials (as expert witnesses) but as consultants to congressional committees, to business organizations, to town governments, to school systems, and in countless other situations.

But once you recognize that experts disagree with one another—as they so often do—you may well wonder why they disagree and what we mean by the term "expert." Unfortunately, a simple definition isn't possible, because "experts" come in several shapes and sizes.

One kind of person who is frequently but incorrectly called an "expert" is simply someone who knows more than you do about something. If you are interested in buying a computer, for example, you may seek "expert" advice from a friend of yours who bought a computer a year ago and has learned something about software. This may strike you as a silly example, but all too often businesses and government agencies become highly impressed with such an "expert" simply because, knowing nothing about a problem themselves, they exaggerate the knowledge of someone who seems to know at least something.

Not long ago, for example, a physician designated as an "expert witness" testified before a congressional committee on abortion that life begins at the moment when an egg is fertilized by a sperm. This is the kind of issue not subject to "expert" opinion because it is not a question of scientific fact; the answer depends on one's definition of "life." A number of more-qualified scientists pointed this out, but many of his hearers took the physician seriously.

Another kind of expert might be called the self-appointed or media-appointed expert. Such a person has usually earned prominence deservedly for his expertness in a specific field but—often as a result of the respect paid him by the public or the media—begins to think of himself as a kind of general-purpose expert, competent and eager to render equally expert opinions on any subject. In addition to William Shockley (see p. 5), a recent example is Dr. Benjamin Spock, whose worldwide acclaim as an expert on child rearing (which, in fact, he was) apparently persuaded him that he was sufficiently expert in politics to campaign for the presidency of the United States. Dr. Spock's campaign was short-lived, but other such "experts" can have long-term influence on public issues. You can protect yourself against "experts'" opinions by recognizing that, if most issues are complex enough to require an expert, most people can't possibly become expert in two unrelated fields.

The third kind of expert is the person who has specialized

in his field and achieved recognition and respect not necessarily from the media but from his colleagues—by winning important professional awards, by writing books and scientific articles, by being appointed to influential positions in his profession. You might think that two such genuine experts, working in the same field, would reach the same conclusions, but actually such experts often disagree. It's not uncommon, in fact, for a congressional committee to hear two experts, apparently equally qualified, flatly contradict each other. In such circumstances, whom should the congressmen (or you) believe?

There are several explanations for the experts' disagreement. To begin with, experts are not always uninfluenced by the point of view of the organization that is supporting their research or paying them salaries or consulting fees. And so it's not surprising that a biologist working for the American Tobacco Institute (which is supported by the industry) disagrees with one working for the U.S. Public Health Service on the relationship between smoking and cancer.

Similarly, when the president establishes a committee of experts to examine an issue, he is quite likely to appoint to it "experts" whose previous work reflects strong agreement with his own views and policies. This is probably why President Reagan's committee to investigate hunger in the United States reported that they found virtually none and another committee, established by Harvard University at about the same time, found a good deal of it.

It would be easy, of course, if we could use a good-guy-vs.-bad-guy approach to decide which expert to believe, but there are other reasons for disagreement. One expert's research design may differ enough from the other's to lead to quite different conclusions. Outsiders who are equally expert may decide that Expert A's design is sounder than Expert B's, but the general public, including members of Congress, can't make this judgment.

Often, too, experts disagree with one another because of genuine uncertainties. Today the only honest answer to the question of whether a chemical that causes cancer in rats will also cause cancer in human beings is "We don't know." Expert A, who is extremely cautious, assumes that it can. Expert B points out that there is no evidence for Expert A's assumption. The choice that the government makes between these conflicting opinions is likely to be based on economics and politics, not on scientific evidence.

One serious problem with expert opinion stems not from the experts themselves but from the media through which we learn what the experts have to say. As we've noted, the media prefer everything they present to be not only dramatic but, because of their limitations of time or space, short and simple. But most significant scientific discoveries, even very important ones, can't be explained in a single column of newspaper space or a two-minute television interview without the loss of some very important details—details that often qualify or limit the discovery and thus make it somewhat less dramatic. This tendency of the media to over-dramatize and oversimplify scientific discoveries has led a significant number of scientists to refuse all interviews and to publish their work in full detail in scientific journals addressed to their colleagues. But this does not prevent journalists from reading—and oversimplifying—the scientific publications.

WORDS, WORDS, WORDS

Even though newspapers have pictures and television is almost entirely a visual medium, the meaning that you get from either depends essentially on words. A full understanding of the meanings that words convey and the feelings they arouse —a subject called *semantics*—requires years of study. But for our purposes two or three basic ideas may be sufficient to put you on your guard against distortion and falsehood.

Nice Words for Not-Nice Things

You probably already know that *euphemisms* are pleasant words or phrases used to describe unpleasant realities—for example, the use of "passed on" instead of "died," or the description of a fat woman as having "a full figure." These euphemisms are harmless enough, because we're all familiar with the reality they describe. But euphemisms become dangerously misleading when they are used to describe an object or an event with which we're not familiar. When, for example, an American military operation is described as a "peace-keeping mission," how many people will recognize it as an armed invasion? In a *New York Times* article on the use of military euphemisms, Caryl Rivers, a professor of journalism at Boston University, puts it this way:

> Today, the more gruesome, the more grotesque the weapon of destruction, the more sanitized the terminology by which it is described.
> In World War II, when we sent out B-29's against Japan, we called it "fire-bombing." It wasn't hard to visualize the great fire storms blowing through the Tokyo streets. Today, our weapons make those incendiary bombs look like a pack of matches. And what do we call them? Intercontinental ballistic missiles and medium-range tactical cruises and multiple-warhead missiles (that is, MIRV's, or multiple independently targetable re-entry vehicles), and the MX. MX sounds like it ought to be a sports car, and MIRV a new Atari game. Since these devices can turn flesh to molten paste in seconds, the use of high-tech lingo for talking about Armageddon is no

accident. . . . The way we talk about something has a great deal to do with the way we think about it.

Often political pressure groups and other organizations adopt names that create a generally favorable impression but conceal their real purposes. A name such as the Committee for Fair Taxation, for example, doesn't tell you that the group's sole purpose is to cut your school budget. The Neighborhood Preservation Committee, whose name suggests tree planting and similar improvements, may, in fact, have been organized for the sole (and illegal) purpose of keeping blacks or other minorities from buying homes in the community. Can you decide, from its name alone, whether or not you would be sympathetic toward a group called People for the American Way of Life?

What'd He Say?

Even when the language used in a message is plain enough, you need to listen (or read the fine print) very carefully to avoid being misled. This is especially true of newspaper advertisements and television commercials. Because the Federal Trade Commission requires advertisers to tell the truth, you are not likely to see or hear grossly misleading claims—though the commission allows a certain amount of exaggeration. But in order to comply with the "truth" requirement, advertisers have learned some rather tricky ways with words.

When the television commercial for a flashlight battery says, "Nothing outshines or outlasts the Energizer!" is it claiming that the Energizer is *better* than other batteries? That's what it would like you to believe—and apparently many people do. Or is it saying that other batteries are no better? Or that they are just as good? This happens to be true, according to tests run by Consumers Union on different batteries of the same type. But clearly this is not the impression the commercial hopes to convey.

When an over-the-counter medicine is advertised as "effective for the temporary relief of symptoms of ———," is it likely to cure anything? Not if you take note of the word "temporary" and if you realize that the relief of symptoms never cures anything, although it may make you feel better —temporarily.

The Federal Trade Commission also requires that television commercials not be deceptive visually. And so, when a color television set or photographs made by a new color camera are advertised, the word "simulated" is flashed on the screen (very briefly) to inform the audience that they are not seeing the real thing. But if the "true-to-life" color is, in fact, simulated, how do you know what the real thing looks like?

Similarly, when an optometrist advertises a special price on contact lenses, many state laws require him to specify whether the price includes the initial examination as well as subsequent checkups, which are especially important for contact lenses. Optometrists usually comply with this by displaying these conditions in writing on the television screen—but so briefly that only speed readers can grasp the message and in such small print that few people needing contact lenses can even make it out.

HOW TO PROTECT YOURSELF

Many people today—usually those with low levels of education—have a broad and unshakable distrust of the media. The reasons for this feeling are several. Some people confuse the messenger with the message—that is, they blame the media because in recent years there has probably been more bad news than good to report. Some people see the media's frequent criticism of government figures as a "conspiracy" by a small group of powerful editors and network executives to discredit the president and his administration.

People with more education don't share this mistrust, recognizing that the media range very widely in quality and reliability and that the *New York Times* and the *National Enquirer* have as little in common as Robert MacNeil of the "MacNeil/Lehrer Newshour" and the person who forecasts the weather on your local television station.

But, as we have seen, all media are, at least to some degree, guilty of distortions and omissions. To some extent you can protect yourself from these by imitating what prudent investors do in the stock market. Instead of risking all their money on the stock of one company, they *diversify*—that is, they buy several stocks in companies that are quite different from one another. If, instead of devoting yourself to the same news program every night or to the same local newspaper, you diversify your reading and listening time among a variety of newspapers, news magazines, and network news programs, you will learn more and you will get a more balanced view of reality.

You can protect yourself further by becoming aware of the kinds of falsehood that you're most likely to encounter regularly in any of the media—and almost everywhere else. These are the subject of the next chapter.

5

Falsehoods—Innocent and Other-wise

Some dogs are black.
I have a black dog.
He's some dog!

As we've noted, the world is not conveniently divided into "good guys," who always tell the truth, and "bad guys," who always lie. Some people—ambitious politicians and their supporters, for example, or overeager advertisers and salespeople—do, of course, create or pass on falsehoods, distortions, or exaggerations because they stand to gain personally from the falsehood. But, as we'll see in this chapter, much—perhaps most—false or inaccurate information is perpetuated by well-meaning people who don't fully understand the issue with which they are dealing or who don't know enough about logic to spot the weaknesses in the arguments that they accept and pass on to others.

As we examine the various errors that damage or destroy the accuracy of what we hear and read, you are likely to recognize that all of us are susceptible to them and that it is more sensible to evaluate an idea on its own merits than on its source. Here are some sources of error that all of us need to watch out for:

IT'S SORT OF LIKE A . . .

One of the best ways to explain an abstract or complex idea is to use *analogy*—that is, to explain the complex idea in terms of something that is similar but simpler and more familiar. If, for example, you are trying to explain to your younger brother why many Mississippi steamboats had boiler explosions, you could compare the boiler explosion to what happens when he blows up a balloon too enthusiastically.

Because they are so useful for both explanation and argument, analogies are encountered almost everywhere—in the classroom, in the media, and in daily conversation. But the trouble with analogies is that the complex and the simple idea are almost never identical—as you've probably noticed from our boiler-balloon comparison. True, both explode when pressure builds up too high. But a balloon is flexible and a boiler is not. A boiler has a safety valve and a balloon does not. An exploding balloon releases harmless air, but a boiler releases scalding steam with destructive force.

More important, the engineer responsible for the boiler knew precisely how much pressure it could withstand, whereas your kid brother had no such specifications when he blew up the balloon. Actually, most steamboat boilers blew up because the engineers deliberately exceeded their pressure limits (sometimes by ordering a crew member to sit on the safety valve) in the hope of breaking speed records —and this is not what usually causes a balloon to burst.

Yet, despite all these differences, the boiler-balloon analogy can be useful in explaining what happens when pressure inside a closed container builds up—provided that the analogy isn't carried too far and that the differences are kept in mind.

Real difficulties arise when the analogy maker or, more usually, the person for whom the analogy is intended is unaware of very significant differences. A friend of yours, for example, may encourage you to take the wheel of a power boat by telling you, "It's just like driving a car." In a general way this is true, in that both power boats and cars are driven by an engine and steered by a wheel. But cars are steered by changing the direction of their front ends, whereas boats are steered by changing the direction of their rear ends; and cars have brakes, whereas boats don't. If your friend doesn't warn you about these differences, you may find yourself neck deep in both water and trouble before you've discovered them for yourself.

To cite another example, when a politician compares the federal government's budget with your family's household budget and points out that, like your family, the government can't "keep on borrowing," he is—intentionally or not—using a misleading analogy. In fact, unlike your family, the government has an almost limitless ability to borrow. In fact, government borrowing can be used very effectively to improve life for many people, whereas family borrowing is often a sign of trouble. And, in fact, governments that borrow heavily can pay off their debts by raising taxes, whereas a family in debt is unlikely to be able to raise its income.

The politician's analogy would have been more accurate had it compared the federal government to a large, successful corporation, most of which are constantly in debt—and may even have a year or two in which they spend a lot more money than they take in. But this analogy would not have given his listeners the negative attitude toward government spending that he intended to create.

Perhaps the most treacherous kind of analogy involves a comparison between the behavior of human beings and that of lower animals. The errors here run in two directions. First, there is the tendency—called *anthropomorphism*—to assume that lower animals behave in a human way. Many cat owners, for example, firmly believe that when their pet rubs itself against their ankles it is expressing affection. The fact is that this rubbing is instinctive, genetically programmed behavior that comes about automatically when the cat is hungry, because early in life this rubbing stimulated the flow of milk through its mother's nipples. The cat rubbing against your ankles doesn't love you in any human sense but sees you as a source of food. In general, lower animals have neither the emotions nor the thought processes of human beings.

On the other hand, it is all too easy to exaggerate the similarity of human beings to lower animals. Human beings are, of course, animals and have many of the same needs, physiology, and reactions as other mammals. This is why the results of animal experiments on diet, drugs, surgery, and learning can often be applied to human beings. But the differences between human beings and other animals are often more striking than the similarities, and these differences may make some analogies questionable if not downright nonsensical.

In a famous experiment, a psychologist observed the behavior of laboratory rats in an enclosed area which quickly became overcrowded as a result of their breeding. When the overcrowding reached a certain level, the rats began to behave in "criminal" ways, stealing or fighting over food, and even eating each other. These results were used by many people to conclude that the overcrowding of people in large cities was the basic cause of crime. But this conclusion is questionable on two grounds. First, human beings have an infinitely greater capacity for learning than laboratory rats— and hence they can learn to get along with one another at close quarters. Second, and more important, research has shown that some of the most overcrowded cities have a lower crime rate than some small towns or sparsely populated rural areas. In short, population density alone is not the cause of crime.

Whenever you encounter an analogy, you need to ask whether it clarifies an idea or oversimplifies it or seriously distorts it. You can do this simply by trying to find important differences between the complex and the simple ideas that make up the analogy. You may not be successful every time, but you may be surprised at how obvious some of these differences are once you begin looking for them.

TRUTH OR CONSEQUENCES?

The state that, for the past ten years, has produced the highest SAT scores in the country is New Hampshire. This information comes not from the New Hampshire state tourist bureau or chamber of commerce, which you might suspect of exaggerating, but from the U.S. Department of Education, which has no reason to extol the virtues of New Hampshire. So we may safely assume that the information is true.

But the question of *why* New Hampshire students outscore everyone else has prompted a lot of different answers. Because New Hampshire ranks the lowest of all fifty states in its budget for education—and forty-eighth in the salaries it pays teachers—some taxpayers seem convinced that its very low budget, which forces schools to get rid of "frills" and concentrate on "basics," is responsible for New Hampshire's high scores. But others argue that, because the state's low-quality schools don't prepare or motivate most students for college entrance, only the children of well-educated and affluent parents take the SAT, and that the normally higher scores of such students inflate the state average.

One high-school principal, on the other hand, insists that the scores are high because "old-fashioned values still exist here." Others, echoing his point, give the credit to strict classroom discipline, small class sizes, and close monitoring of attendance. But some say the SAT scores are artificially high because the state has an unusually low proportion of poor minority students, who lower the averages because they often do badly on a test designed primarily for middle-class white students. Still others argue that the high scores are produced by the children of highly educated professionals who work in the high-tech industries near Boston but who live just across the Massachusetts state line because New Hampshire levies no state income tax.

In theory, any one of these explanations may be right—or wrong—although it's also possible that several of them play a part. Or perhaps the real reason is that the incredibly cold New Hampshire winters keep students indoors—and studying! In any event, finding the right answer (or answers) would involve some rather difficult research and not the hunches and guesswork of people with various interests.

The New Hampshire case illustrates a very common phenomenon: when confronted by facts, we all tend to try to discover their cause. That is, when A is true, we try to identify a B (which is also true) as its cause. But our choice of B rather than C or D or E (which are also true and may be equally plausible) usually reflects our prejudices and interests rather than scientific logic.

Further examples of this kind of error are easy enough to find. Phyllis Schlafly, an opponent of the women's liberation movement, has noted that the rise in illegitimate teenage pregnancies (A) began shortly after courses in sex education (B) were widely introduced into the public schools, and her conclusion is that B caused A. Of course, nobody with scientific training would share her conclusion, but she presumably influenced many of her followers.

Many educators, noting that the decline in SAT verbal scores began in 1962, the year by which most families had acquired television sets, blamed the decline entirely on television viewing. Other educators identify other causes, but there is almost no way of proving who is right.

This kind of thinking has a Latin label—the *post hoc, ergo propter hoc* (*after* this, therefore *because of* this) fallacy. It cautions against our assuming that because A was *followed* by B, B therefore *caused* A.

WHAT'S MISSING FROM THIS PICTURE?

Because our society, like any modern society, is extremely complex, almost any change or innovation—whether it's a new law against drunken driving, a cure for a previously incurable disease, or the introduction of computers to handle your bank account—has a very complex set of consequences, some of which are almost certain to be undesirable. Some of these undesirable consequences may be trivial and may affect only a few people, but others may be so serious as to make the change inadvisable or downright dangerous.

Sometimes these undesirable consequences are overlooked by people who "can't see the forest for the trees"; sometimes they are deliberately concealed by people who stand to gain personally from the change. But sometimes they simply can't be foreseen, even by the ablest and best-intentioned people. A few examples will make this clear.

Many citizens, outraged by the deaths and injuries caused by drunken drivers, regularly propose very stiff penalties— revocation of license or a mandatory prison term—for anyone convicted of driving while intoxicated. But these same people overlook, in their righteous anger, the fact that most prisons today are dangerously overcrowded, that proposals for additional prisons are regularly turned down by the voters, and that imprisoning a drunken driver may cause him to lose his job and may thus penalize his wife and children.

They overlook, too, the fact that many drivers whose licenses have been revoked continue to drive without them. And they are probably unaware that most of the drunken drivers involved in fatal accidents are not law-abiding citizens who have had one drink too many but alcoholics who are not likely to be deterred or cured by stiffer penalties.

Perhaps this is why many legislators have hesitated to make the laws more severe—and why those states that have done so find that, after a very short period of improvement, drunken driving becomes as common as it was before the new laws. Yet a campaign for new laws that will "lock up drunken drivers and throw the key away" comes up year after year because the urgent need of the citizens and their legislators "to take some action" seems to prevent them from considering all the relevant information.

Almost every new law that is proposed has supporters and opponents, each of which either fails or refuses to recognize the other side's arguments. Let's look, for example, at the "bottle bill"—a law that would require a deposit on all beverage containers in order to encourage users to return them to the store instead of littering the landscape with them. This law has been passed by a few states, but in many others the beverage industry is fighting it vigorously and the environmentalists are supporting it just as vigorously.

The beverage industry argues that the expenses that storekeepers have in handling and storing the returned empties will raise the prices of beverages and that factories now producing throwaway bottles and cans will have to lay off many of their workers. But this argument overlooks—perhaps deliberately—the environmentalists' claim that the retailers can earn interest on the customers' deposits and that the state (that is, the taxpayers) no longer has to pay its highway crews to pick up the thousands of cans and bottles discarded along roads and highways—a cost that Michigan (which has such a law) estimates at about thirty cents each.

The environmentalists, for their part, admit that a bottle bill may cause some unemployment among workers who produce disposable containers or clean up the highways, but they point out that new jobs will be created for people who handle and transport the returnable containers. They overlook, however, the fact that these new jobs will not necessarily be filled by the laid-off workers from the manufacturing plants and highway cleanup crews.

Which side is right in this battle? At the moment, nobody knows, because not enough information is available from the few states that have passed these laws. In some of them, prices have gone up, but not necessarily *as a result* of the new laws.

Sometimes, as we have said, the consequences of an innovation simply can't be foreseen, because they don't show up immediately. When it was first introduced, the birth-control pill was welcomed as a medical miracle, because it proved far more effective in preventing unwanted pregnancies than any of the methods it replaced. Only after it was in widespread use did doctors become aware of two undesirable side effects. First, the pill has caused severe medical problems in a small number of women who use it. Second, and perhaps more serious, it has caused a huge increase in venereal disease because, unlike one very popular birth-control method that it replaced, it offers no protection against venereal disease.

As you can see, all three of these changes—drunk-driving laws, bottle bills, and the birth-control pill—have been proposed or adopted with good intentions, but all three have undesirable "side effects." When such side effects are concealed or overlooked, or are impossible to anticipate, problems are sure to arise. But what if some undesirable consequences *can* be foreseen? Or what if they are recognized promptly—as in the case of the birth-control pill? How do we decide whether the advantages outweigh them or not? Actually, there is a technique, known as *cost-benefit analysis,* which lets us calculate the costs—that is, the undesirable consequences—and weigh them against a calculation of the benefits.

The calculation of cost-benefits is easy enough to understand if your doctor tells you that what you thought was indigestion is actually acute appendicitis and that you need an operation immediately. The "cost" of such an operation, aside from the money paid to the surgeon and the hospital, is the less-than-2-percent risk that you will die as a result of the anesthetic. The "benefit," on the other hand, is the prevention of almost certain death from appendicitis. Here it's quite obvious, without the need for mathematical computation, that the benefits outweigh the costs.

In the case of the birth-control pill, precise and reliable cost-benefit statistics are available but they are likely to be interpreted differently by each individual. Because the pill is the most reliable form of birth control, the woman who feels that avoiding pregnancy (the "benefit") is very important will risk the side effects of the pill (the "cost"), especially after the doctor reassures her that the chances of a woman's dying of the side effects of the pill are lower than her chances of dying of the complications of pregnancy or childbirth.

But other methods of birth control, readily available, are less effective in preventing pregnancies (that is, their "benefit" is lower) but are less hazardous to a woman's health (and so their "cost" is lower, too). Which method a woman chooses depends on how important it is to avoid pregnancy. If she wants the most reliable form of birth control (high "benefit"), she is likely to choose the pill and pay the high "cost" of possible side effects. If she is less concerned about pregnancy, she is likely to choose a method that is lower in cost.

But often the cost-benefit ratio is impossible to calculate because it can't be reduced to mathematical terms. Statisticians estimate with a high degree of certainty, for example, that laws requiring the use of seat belts in automobiles would prevent about 10,000 deaths and perhaps 150,000 injuries each year, even though not everybody would obey the law. But only one state has such a law—apparently because most legislators feel that the cost of forcing people to use seat belts is higher than the benefit in terms of the number of deaths and injuries that might be prevented. In this case, obviously, neither the cost nor the benefit can be expressed in numbers.

What should you do, then, when you're asked to choose sides on an issue—especially when the cost-benefits are not clear? Your best course is to recognize that *every proposal* or innovation has costs as well as benefits—that there is no perfect solution to any problem. When a friend urges you to support one side and enthusiastically describes its benefits, choose the other side, at least for the moment, in an effort to discover the costs that your friend is overlooking or concealing.

IT OUGHT TO WORK—BUT DOES IT?

Often people propose or support a program because common sense convinces them that "it ought to work." But, as we saw in Chapter 2, common sense can be a treacherous guide. The argument that the death penalty deters people from murder is a good example of the use of common sense without enough reliable information.

Surely it seems logical that anyone planning a murder would have second thoughts if he knew that he would be put to death if he were caught. But this kind of logic is based on three rather questionable assumptions: (1) that most murderers plan their murder in advance, (2) that they seriously consider the probability of being caught, and (3) that a death sentence is more of a deterrent than a long prison sentence.

The facts, unfortunately, apparently fail to support these assumptions. Criminologists who have made careful studies of the deterrent effects of the death penalty—by comparing homicide rates in two similar states, one with the death penalty and one without, or by monitoring the homicide rate in a state before and after it abolished the death penalty—have been unable to find any evidence that it is an effective deterrent. In fact, the noted criminologist William J. Bowers, in his book *Legal Homicide*, argues that the death penalty actually *increases* the homicide rate because it permits some people to feel that they have a right to punish others in the same way that the state does—by killing them.

The question of *why* the death penalty doesn't work can't be answered with certainty, but criminologists who have studied convicted murderers suggest several possibilities. First, contrary to what television shows us, probably more than 85 percent of murders are committed not by hit men or bank robbers but by ordinary human beings, who—because they are either drunk or in a fit of rage—kill a friend or relative without intending to. And even criminals involved in armed robbery kill their victims out of panic rather than intentionally. Murderers who don't intend to commit murder, or who are drunk, panicked, or insanely angry, can hardly be expected to weigh the consequences. As for the death penalty as a threat, a number of murderers facing the choice between the death sentence and life imprisonment have asked for execution.

But, you may ask, if the death penalty doesn't work, why do voters still urge that it be kept or restored? Social scientists suggest three reasons. First, many people, unaware of the research or the reasoning we've referred to, sincerely believe that the death penalty is a deterrent. Second, when people become uncomfortable because the "rules" of society are changing rapidly and they feel that "everybody is getting away with all sorts of things," the death penalty gives them some reassurance that society still stands ready to punish "bad" behavior. Lastly, the death penalty serves as an expression of "revenge" for society as a whole. But because people are often unaware of the real sources of their anxieties, and because "an eye for an eye and a tooth for a tooth" is not a sentiment that people like to acknowledge, the argument that the death penalty is a deterrent is still widely used.

Murder is something you probably don't think about very often, but driving is—and your high-school course in driver education provides us with another example of the danger of using common sense unaccompanied by good information.

Surely it would seem logical that if young people are going to drive cars, being taught to drive properly by a driving expert would help them avoid accidents and traffic tickets. This logic was so compelling that almost every high school set up a driver-education program long before the federal government made it mandatory, and insurance companies began offering premium discounts to young drivers who had passed such a course.

It was not until such courses had gone on for some thirty years that scientists studying highway safety began to question whether in fact they did any good—that is, whether students who passed the course were safer or better drivers than those who were taught to drive by parents or friends. After some extensive and careful studies, the researchers concluded that the typical high-school course in driver education does little or nothing to produce safer drivers but that, in fact, it probably increases the overall accident toll for young drivers by allowing them to be licensed sooner than they would be if they had not taken the course.

Later in this chapter, we'll look at the reasons why the research studies successfully contradicted the common-sense conclusion that driver education courses were "a good idea." At the moment, however, you may be asking, "Why, if these experiments give us good scientific evidence, do schools continue to offer courses in driver education?"

There are several answers to this question. First, whether or not they produce *safe* drivers, these courses free parents from the responsibility of teaching their children to drive and risking the fenders of the family car in the process. Second, the automobile manufacturers support driver education by lending cars for use in the course because the more young drivers licensed, the more cars (and repair parts) they are likely to sell. Third, the teachers of driver-education courses, either because they were unaware of the research or because they were eager to retain their jobs, lobbied successfully to persuade the U.S. Congress to require high schools to teach driver education even after the scientific evidence proved that it had no effect on safety.

If you conclude that scientific evidence often comes off a poor second to voter sentiment, business interests, and other considerations, you won't be far wrong. But this is most likely to happen when common sense—for instance, the notion that a course in driver education *should* improve driving skill—supports a wrong conclusion.

Often you may feel uncomfortable in challenging an idea or a program that seems obviously sensible or logical. Bear in mind, though, that if everyone always felt this way, we would still be sure that the earth is flat.

IS THE DIFFERENCE A REAL ONE?

Because the growth of plants depends on the quality of the soil they grow in and the amount of light and water they receive, botanists who want to compare the productivity of two varieties of corn, for example, will take care to grow them under "controlled" conditions—that is, to plant both varieties in precisely the same kind of soil and to give them identical amounts of light and water. Only in this way can they be sure that any differences in productivity are due to differences between the two varieties and not to differences in the conditions under which they were grown.

This need for "controls" may strike you as too obvious to need discussion, but the fact is that you will encounter—in editorials, in advertisements, and in conversations—a great many statements based on comparisons in which no controls have been used. And when comparisons are uncontrolled, they are just as meaningless as a comparison between two varieties of corn when one of them has been grown under ideal conditions and the other starved for fertilizer, light, and water.

It was the lack of controls that made the research investigators question whether driver-education courses actually delivered what they promised. These scientists acknowledged that students who passed driver-education courses had fewer accidents than those who didn't, but they doubted that the course was the *cause* of the difference. They suspected, instead, that there might be differences between students who took driver-education courses and those who didn't—and that these differences in the students themselves might account for the differences in their driving records.

The scientists took several steps to verify their suspicions. First, by carefully comparing students who did and did not take the course, they found several differences between the two groups—in academic performance, in college plans, and in family income. These differences, they found, could account for (1) the likelihood that the student would choose to take driver education and (2) the likelihood that the student would have a good driving record. In short, the course itself did not appear to be a *cause* of the better driving. Instead, the kind of student who would be likely to be a careful driver was also likely to take the course.

To confirm these findings, the scientists then conducted a second experiment. Instead of allowing students to choose freely whether or not to take driver education, they divided students into two groups, one of which was required to take driver education and the other not permitted to. Because the investigators took care to match the two groups carefully in terms of academic standing, college plans, and family background, any difference in their subsequent driving records would necessarily be due to the course itself. When the driving records of these two groups were compared, the conclusion was that the course made virtually no difference— certainly not enough to justify its costs to the taxpayers on grounds that it taught students to drive safely.

"But if driver-education courses don't produce safer drivers," you may ask, "why do the insurance companies continue to offer premium discounts to students who have passed them?" There are two answers to this question. First, although driver-education courses don't *produce* safer drivers, they are reliable *indicators* of safe driving because, as we've seen, students who choose the course are, in fact, likely to be safer drivers than those who don't, even though the course had nothing to do with the difference. Second, insurance companies make money on these policies, even when the premium is discounted, and encouraging driver-education courses helps get young drivers licensed early and thus increases the number of policies the companies will sell.

When a new drug is being tested, controls become especially important to isolate the effects of the drug. It's not sufficient to have two groups of similar patients, one of which gets the drug and the other doesn't, because merely taking the drug may have psychological effects that can be mistaken for pharmacological ones. For this reason, each group receives "medication." One group gets the drug to be tested, the other a "placebo"—a harmless sugar pill—and neither group is told which pill it is taking.

In addition, in order to prevent bias on the part of the researcher (who might, if he is the developer of the drug, see more improvement in the dosed patients than in the placebo group), the person who examines the patients after treatment is not told which group each patient belongs to. This is called a "double-blind" experiment, and it is the only acceptable form of control for many kinds of research.

Controls are essential not only to ensure that two groups being compared are in fact comparable but also to make sure that comparisons between two time periods make sense. When you ask for a larger allowance, for example, and your parents tell you that at your age they got only three dollars a week, you might point out that: (1) twenty-five years ago each dollar could buy almost three times what it can buy today; and (2) you may be expected to spend your allowance on a number of items (lunches, for example, or school supplies) that their parents provided for them. Unless your parents "control" for changes such as these, their argument won't carry much weight—even though they may very well win it!

ONE FOR ALL AND ALL FOR ONE

One of the problems with the media, as we noted in Chapter 4, was their tendency to focus on a single unusual case. The single unusual case is, of course, generally interesting precisely because it is so different from the ordinary, humdrum majority, but often advertisers, politicians, and others who are trying to sell us a product or a point of view cite one unusual case (sometimes real, sometimes imaginary) in the hope that we'll overlook its uniqueness and assume it to be typical.

Many people, for example, on the basis of a politician's account of one welfare mother whom he says he saw driving a Cadillac, seem to think that *most* welfare mothers own Cadillacs or are otherwise undeserving of welfare payments. Organizations that help the handicapped, to cite another example, may point with justifiable pride to the cerebral-palsy victim who became a university president, but this may give many people the impression that *all* cerebral-palsy victims could achieve distinguished careers "if they'd only try hard," overlooking the fact that a very significant proportion of cerebral-palsy victims are mentally retarded.

A magazine or newspaper article about a woman who has been appointed to the U.S. Supreme Court is unlikely to mention that *most* women still rank significantly below men in terms of either earnings or job status. Sellers of diet pills show us "before" and "after" photographs of the woman who lost fifty pounds in two weeks but they don't tell us, of course, how many of their customers lost only one pound or found the pills completely worthless.

None of the examples we've just cited is necessarily untrue. The problem lies in what they suggest—or in what people who read or hear them conclude. This use of one or two cases to suggest a general rule is called the *anecdotal method* and it is totally rejected by trained scientists. But the reverse of this—the use of large numbers of cases to suggest that their experience is true for *everyone*—is equally misleading, as in the suggestion, for example, that aspirin, because it's effective for most people, is sure to be effective for you.

If a scientist who is testing the effectiveness of a new medication, or a surgeon trying out a new surgical procedure, discovers that it works on 100 percent of his patients, not only will he be suspected by his colleagues but he will be suspicious himself. People differ so widely in so many respects that not only a surgical operation but most other experiences —a college education, seeing a movie, a trip to Europe, the divorce of their parents—will not have the same effect on all of them.

Since the scientist or the surgeon can't expect effectiveness in 100 percent of cases, what percentage *should* he expect if he is to claim that his new treatment is successful—51 percent? 75 percent? 90 percent? This is too complex a question for us to answer here, but it does suggest the importance of numbers—the subject of the next chapter.

=6=

Statistics Prove . . . (or) Is There Safety in Numbers?

And that's the news from Lake Wobegon . . .
where all the children are above average.
—*Garrison Keillor*

Finding flaws in supposedly factual statements is, as we've seen, not terribly hard. But what if the statement is backed up by "statistical evidence"? What if someone tells you, for example, that although 54 percent of all high-school graduates enter college, only 40 percent of these incoming freshmen actually graduate four years later? What should this tell you about your own college plans?

If, like a good many of us, you haven't enjoyed your math courses, almost any statement that includes statistics may make you feel uncomfortable. And this is why many people react to a statistical statement in one of two ways: either they accept it in blind faith, because they don't know how to evaluate it critically, or they reject it completely—not because they see flaws in the statistics but simply because they've heard somewhere that "There are liars, damned liars, and statisticians."

Statistics are not good or bad, honest or fraudulent, in themselves. They are nothing more than sets of numbers that can give us definite information about people or events. They can tell us, for example, that Democrats outnumber Republicans by more than three to one (but that Republicans are more likely to go to the polls on Election Day)—or that the divorce rate has been going up for the past twenty years and today one out of three first marriages ends in divorce. (They can tell us, too, that people who marry young are most likely to divorce!)

Like any other man-made device—knives, jet engines, or printing presses, for instance—statistics can be used for good purposes or bad, depending on the motives and skills of the people using them. If you learn enough about how statistics are put together, however, you can deal with a statistical argument as comfortably as you do with an expression of opinion. You can judge for yourself whether a set of numbers tossed at you in a television commercial, a newspaper story, an editorial, or an argument with a friend is sound, acceptable evidence or a dishonest attempt to change your mind about an issue, a political candidate, or a commercial product.

THE IMPORTANCE OF NUMBERS

As you've known for a long time, there are many things that don't make sense unless they have numbers attached to them. You can't tell, for example, how well you did on a test unless you know your score, and even your score won't be meaningful unless you know *two other numbers:* the minimum passing score and the number of students who scored higher or lower than you. You can't decide whether you are fat or skinny unless you know *three numbers:* your weight, your height, and your age, so that you can compare your weight with the weights of other males or females of your height and age. (If you take these three numbers to your family doctor, he or she will be able to tell you, by consulting a statistical table, what percent of Americans your age are shorter or skinnier than you.)

AVERAGE HEIGHTS AND WEIGHTS FOR BOYS AND GIRLS

Age	BOYS Height (in.)	BOYS Weight (lb.)	GIRLS Height (in.)	GIRLS Weight (lb.)
10	54.1	69.3	54.4	71.8
11	56.4	77.8	57.0	81.5
12	58.9	87.7	59.6	91.6
13	61.6	99.1	61.9	101.6
14	64.2	111.9	63.1	110.8
15	66.5	125.0	63.7	118.3
16	68.3	136.9	63.9	123.2
17	69.4	146.2	64.2	125.0
18	69.6	151.9	64.4	124.8

Source: National Academy of Sciences

Checking your own height and weight against this table may change your mind about how "fat" or "skinny" you are, but before becoming either elated or depressed, bear in mind that these figures are *averages,* that there is a good deal of individual variation, and that genetic differences among ethnic groups cause differences in height and weight. Hispanics and Asians, for example, are likely to fall below these averages on both measures.

It is because statistics make information precise and reliable that scientists take them so seriously. Believing, as they do, that anything "real" must be countable or measurable, scientists rarely make or accept a statement that is not backed up by statistical evidence. But this kind of evidence is not used only by scientists to exchange information among themselves. It is just as useful for planning all sorts of public and private activities, and for getting information to the public in order to change incorrect ideas and beliefs.

Many voters, for example, in their eagerness to reduce their taxes, vote to abolish programs providing free prenatal care for pregnant women who can't afford to pay for it—especially since most of the voters don't benefit personally from such programs. They might change their votes, however, if they saw statistics showing that tax-supported hospital services for premature babies and other problems resulting from the lack of prenatal care will cost them many times more than the programs that prevent them.

This doesn't mean, of course, that statistical information always changes people's opinions—especially if those opinions happen to be widespread and comfortable. Changing one's opinion, as you may know, can be a painful process— and this may be why so many people dislike or mistrust statistics.

The fact remains, however, that most people, even though they may be reluctant to change their opinions, will cheerfully assume that statistics are "really scientific" and therefore "must be true." And this creates two problems. Some editorial writers, politicians, advertisers, or salesmen, whose motive is not to give you precise knowledge but rather to persuade you to make decisions or choices that benefit them, deliberately use misleading statistics in the hope of adding "scientific" authority to their arguments. And some of these misleading statistics are simply passed along innocently by other people—textbook writers, teachers, debaters—who are impressed by them but don't have the training needed to evaluate them critically.

How, then, can you decide which statistics are trustworthy and which are not? To learn how to detect the very subtle flaws in some of the statistics put together by highly sophisticated statisticians, you would need much more information than this book can give you. But—fortunately for us—most misleading statistics are *not* produced by capable statisticians.

Therefore you can detect their weaknesses by asking some simple questions. In this chapter, we'll look at the questions you ought to ask. And we'll illustrate the reasons behind each of the questions by analyzing familiar, everyday statements or arguments containing the weaknesses that your questions can expose.

CAN IT BE MEASURED OR COUNTED?

Because every statistic is a number, statistics can deal only with phenomena that can be measured or counted. Thus, by using income-tax reports, Census Bureau reports, and information from the Bureau of Labor Statistics, we can assemble fairly accurate statistics on how much money Americans earn (in dollars per year) or how long they work (in hours per week). Using birth and death certificates and government health reports, we can get figures on how long people live (in years) and what they die of (in numbers of cases of each fatal illness). By counting the number of new car registrations, we can discover how many automobiles are bought each year. If the basic information behind these statistics is accurate, the statistics themselves will be trustworthy.

But often we may be interested in something that can't be directly measured or counted, and in such situations we have to rely on indirect measurement. Sometimes these indirect measurements are ingenious as well as logical. The directors of an art museum, for example, wanting to know which of two paintings in the museum was more interesting to visitors, obviously had no way of measuring "interest." What they did was to compare the length of life of the floor tiles directly in front of each picture, assuming that the floor tiles wore out more quickly in front of the picture that attracted the larger number of visitors—or visitors who stood in front of the picture for the longer period of time.

But very often indirect measures are not reliable, as the following statement demonstrates: *Americans are certainly becoming more religious. Just look at how rapidly church attendance is increasing!*

Because intensity of religious feeling can't be measured in numbers, it would seem logical to look at church attendance, which *can* be measured. But don't some people go to church to meet their neighbors or to impress their friends rather than to pray to God, and can't some deeply religious people express their religion at home? The figures that show increasing church attendance may be entirely accurate. The question is whether they really measure what they are assumed to measure.

You may have heard someone say: *Marriages must be mostly unhappy these days. Just look at the way the divorce rate has been going up. Divorce now breaks up one out of three marriages.*

Here the divorce rate, which is easily measurable, is being used as an indirect measure of happiness in marriage, which is not directly measurable. Before you accept this indirect measure as logical, you need to think about factors *other than happiness in marriage* that may account for changes in the divorce rate. Here are just a few of them:

- Today more people think that divorce is acceptable and fewer people think that it is shameful or sinful than they did thirty years ago.
- Today couples are marrying at an earlier age, and couples who marry young are more likely to divorce.

- The condition of the economy has a lot to do with the divorce rate. When times are good, the divorce rate goes up.
- Today more people expect that marriage will be happy, and so they are more willing to break up an unhappy marriage in the hope of finding a happier one.
- There is no evidence that all couples who *don't* divorce are happy in their marriages. Many unhappy couples remain together "for the sake of the children."

When a television commercial tells you that the 1984 Fords are "more reliable" than competing makes, the statement is based on the number of owner complaints recorded during the first three months of ownership. Would you agree that this is a reliable measure of reliability?

When you are offered any kind of statistic, then, ask yourself whether it is direct or indirect and, if it is indirect, whether it offers acceptable evidence for the conclusion it supposedly supports. Your community newspaper may proudly point to the increasing daily number of visitors to an art museum as evidence of a growing interest in art. But before you accept this evidence, ask yourself whether the sudden enthusiasm for art may have anything to do with the fact that a nearby public restroom was recently closed down.

Although indirect measurement can be tricky, at least it is based on something that can, in fact, be measured. But obviously dishonest people often try to give scientific respectability to unscientific statements by using numbers that are based on no measurement at all. In one form or another, you've probably heard this statement as part of a television commercial: *Dazzler toothpaste gets your teeth 32 percent whiter.*

Obviously a fourteen-pound weight is seven times heavier than a two-pound weight, and a 420-page book is seven times longer than a 60-page book. In both these cases we are dealing with measurable units (pounds and pages). But how can one measure a shade of white?

The 32 percent nicely illustrates the ploy of using a precise but meaningless measurement to persuade people that the information is scientific. The classic example is the original advertising claim that Ivory Soap is $99^{44}/_{100}$ percent pure. This was dreamed up by an advertising writer who later admitted that he concocted the figure because he thought it sounded "more scientific" than the equally meaningless "100 percent pure."

IS EVERYBODY HERE OR ARE SOME PEOPLE ABSENT?

Almost all statistics are based not directly on what actually happens in real life but on *reports* of what happens. And so no statistics can be more accurate than the report or records on which they're based.

Some records—of births, for example—are likely to be quite accurate because very few babies are born without the help of a nurse or a doctor, who is required by law to file a birth certificate. Besides, there are so many advantages and so few disadvantages to having a birth certificate that almost nobody deliberately avoids filing one. Similarly, records of automobile registrations are fairly accurate because very few people risk driving a car without plates on it.

But many other records tend to leave out certain kinds of people or events. Suppose someone says, for example: *The suicide rate in Denmark is much higher than in the United*

States, so life in Denmark must be much worse than it is here. Offhand, you would think that death certificates (which specify the cause of death) would be as accurate as birth certificates, and that therefore the comparison between the United States and Denmark is a fair one. But this is not true with respect to suicide. In Denmark, suicide is a socially acceptable way of dying, and no Dane about to commit suicide will try to conceal evidence of it, nor will any doctor try to substitute a more acceptable cause of death on the death certificate. In the United States, on the other hand, suicide has always been regarded as a shameful (even a criminal) act, and so some people commit suicide by having an automobile or gun "accident," and many physicians will change "suicide" to something less shameful when they enter the cause of death on the certificate. Therefore, although the Danish suicide rate *may* be higher than the American, the statistics (based on death certificates) do not prove it.

Of course, even if the suicide rate in Denmark is higher than it is in the United States, this difference in no way proves that life is worse in Denmark.

You have probably often heard the statement: *Teenagers are terrible drivers. They have three times as many accidents as older people.*

Bearing in mind that accident statistics are based on accident reports filed by the police, you can ask yourself whether the difference in accident frequency may be due not to differences in driving but to the possibility that accidents involving teenagers are more likely to be reported. In fact, this happens to be true.

If your father has a minor collision with somebody, he may offer to pay for the damages on the spot or ask to be billed for them, because he is fairly sure that if he files an insurance claim his next year's premiums will go up. If the other driver trusts him, there will be no police report and his accident will never become a statistic. On the other hand, if you, as a young driver, had the same collision, the other driver might assume you were financially irresponsible and would there-fore call the police to report the accident officially. This is one reason—though not the only one—why the statistics for every state show that teenagers have more accidents than adults. Certainly they have more *reported* accidents.

The likelihood that a set of statistical records will be seriously incomplete is greater than most people think. Even the U.S. Census statistics, which are supposed to include everybody, are by no means complete. Several million illegal aliens evade the census takers for fear of being deported, and many other people—usually those with low incomes—suspect the census takers of being welfare investigators and hence avoid being counted.

Crime statistics, with the exception of homicide, are even less reliable. In some cities, where residents have a poor opinion of the police force and feel that reporting a crime would be a waste of time, as many as 80 percent of burglaries and robberies are never reported and therefore don't appear in the records.

Sometimes, on the other hand, you can't be sure whether the statistics you are offered are inaccurate because they *omit* cases or because they *include* cases that should not be in-cluded. We've just noted that crime statistics are often in-accurate because they don't include unreported crimes. But there is another reason for their inaccuracy. When criminals are caught by the police, the promise of getting a lighter sentence if they "come clean" may motivate them to confess to a number of crimes that they did not commit—and thus the resulting statistics make the police look more efficient than they really are.

Let's look at a statement that you'll encounter frequently in newspapers and on television news programs: *The latest figures show that unemployment has risen to 9.5 percent.*

Whatever the current unemployment rate, the figures are based on reports from state unemployment offices, where people come to look for jobs or to collect their unemployment checks. These figures may make the unemployment situation look *better* than it actually is because they don't include people whose unemployment checks have run out and those who have given up hope of looking for work. On the other hand, they may make the situation look *worse* than it is if a great many married housewives decide, because of good economic conditions or because of the women's liberation movement, to start looking for a job even though they have never worked before. We may be able to guess at whether the figures overestimate or underestimate the unemployment situation, but we can never be absolutely sure.

So when somebody says "Let's look at the record," be sure you know how the record was made.

ARE YOU GETTING A WRONG NUMBER?

Earlier in this chapter, you learned to be suspicious of indirect measurements—that is, numbers that don't directly measure the subject in which you're interested. Sometimes, though, statistics do present what looks like a direct measurement, and your problem is to decide whether it really means anything. Let's take an advertising slogan: *Whizbang Airlines: the company that has flown one billion miles without an accident.*

Should this statistic convince you that Whizbang is a safe airline? You could, of course, look at the Federal Aviation Authority reports, which list the number of crashes each airline has experienced per million miles. But is the line with the lowest number of crashes necessarily the safest? You won't think so if you realize that almost all air crashes occur within minutes of takeoff or landing and therefore that an aircraft that flies 3,000 miles nonstop from Washington to San Francisco has not much more likelihood of crashing than one that flies 70 miles from one town to another. As you'll see in the FAA reports, the smaller airlines have more crashes per million miles than the large ones, but is this because they use careless pilots and unsafe equipment or because they make shorter trips and have many more landings and takeoffs than the big companies?

Your driver-education teacher may tell you that: *Male drivers have about four times as many accidents as female drivers, and they get more than four times as many tickets.* If you look at the driving records of 1,000 males and 1,000 females, you'll find that this statement is correct. But should you be looking at the number of *drivers* or at the number of *miles* they drive? Once you discover that males drive about four times as many miles per year as females, you might reasonably conclude that this gives them four times as much opportunity to have accidents or accumulate tickets as females, not that they are any worse drivers. Even a comparison of mileage isn't the whole story. Males are more likely to drive when the weather or road conditions are dangerous. Females do much of their driving on slow-speed shopping trips.

In short, make sure the numbers you're given are the right ones for the conclusions they're supposed to prove.

ARE YOU GETTING ENOUGH NUMBERS?

As you saw at the beginning of this chapter, knowing your score on a test doesn't tell you very much unless you know the passing score. In some situations, a single number can be downright misleading. If you were to see the newspaper headline: NEW YORK CITY SCENE OF 1,600 MURDERS THIS YEAR, you might decide that life would be safer, if not happier, in Houston, Texas, where only about 450 people are murdered each year. But a moment's thought would lead you to recognize that New York's population is about five times as large as Houston's and that your chance of being murdered depends not on the *raw number* of murders but on the *rate;* that is, the number of murders per 100,000 population. Once you compare the two cities on the basis of their homicide rates, you find that Houston has the highest large-city rate in the country and that New York, despite all you may have heard, ranks about twelfth among American cities. The raw number is high in New York only because the city has a huge population. But the current "murder capital" in terms of homicide *rate* is the small town of Odessa, Texas.

If you read or hear anything that gives you only raw numbers, don't be impressed. Ask for (or try to calculate) the *rate,* because the rate tells you the number of happenings (whether homicides or divorces or high-school graduations) divided by the number of people who might have been involved in such happenings.

The rate that you're already familiar with, of course, is the percentage, which tells you the number of happenings *per hundred people.* If you hear that 25 percent of the students in your school smoke marijuana, you know that this means twenty-five students out of every hundred, or one out of every four. This is much more meaningful than a statement

that seventy-two students in your school smoke marijuana—
especially if you don't know the actual size of the student
body.

On the other hand, although rates are much more reliable
than raw numbers, they can easily mislead you unless you
remain alert to several problems.

The first of these problems has to do with percentages.
Because percentages always mean "per 100," we are apt to
assume that they describe at least 100 cases and probably
more. When, for example, you read that *50 percent of
American families have incomes of less than $20,000 a year,*
you can be reasonably sure that this statement covers a very
large number of families. But, as you know, "three out of
four" of anything can be expressed as "75 percent," and
hence, when you see an advertisement claiming that *75 percent of veterinarians recommend Micesoufflé cat food,* you
know that the advertiser would like you to think that he
interviewed thousands of veterinarians. But you know also
that he could make the same statement after interviewing
only four—if he were lucky enough to find three Micesoufflé
enthusiasts among them. Percentages based on small numbers can never be trusted.

Whenever you see a percentage, think carefully about the
realities behind it. When, for example, your state governor
announces that there will be a *7-percent cost-of-living
increase awarded to all state employees,* this may strike you
as very fair until you realize that the governor's $30,000-a-
year administrative assistant will get a raise of $2,100, while
the road-repair worker will get 7 percent of $11,000, even
though both of them have to pay the same price for a quart
of milk or a gallon of gas.

The basis on which the percentage is calculated is especially important when percentages are used to express changes. If, for example, Toyota announces that it had a 6-percent increase in car sales last year and Renault announces a 12-percent increase, which company has more to cheer about? Renault would seem the obvious choice unless you knew that Toyota's 6-percent increase amounted to almost 3,400 cars while Renault's 12-percent increase represented only about 1,650 cars. It's always easier for the smaller company to show the larger percentage increase.

Another problem—this one common to all rates—is that even when they are accurate they may lead you to conclusions that are not justified. Suppose your school paper runs a headline: 85 PERCENT OF THIS YEAR'S GRADUATES ADMITTED TO COLLEGE, and suppose the story under the headline goes on to point out that your school has the highest percentage of college entrants in the city and that one of the high schools across town sends only 15 percent of its graduates on to college. These figures are probably accurate, but what conclusion can you draw from them?

that the teachers at your school are better?
that the students at your school are brighter?
that your school curriculum encourages more students to continue their education?
that your guidance counselor has "pull" with college admissions officers?
all of the above?
none of the above?

The fact is that the likelihood of your entering college depends far more on the education and income of your parents than it does on any of the possibilities we've suggested above, and that the C-average student who has well-to-do, college-educated parents is two to four times more likely to enter college than the brilliant student whose low-income parents dropped out of high school. Only if your school and the school across town have exactly the same kind of student body (which is highly unlikely) can you begin thinking about the quality of the teachers or the brightness of the students.

The question "What do rate differences really tell me?" is one that you should apply to all rates. Rates in themselves only *measure* differences; they never tell you what lies behind the differences. If you read, for example, that *Alaska schools spend more money per pupil than schools in any other state,* you may understandably jump to the conclusion that the quality of education in Alaska must be splendid, because you're aware that high salaries attract good teachers and that science laboratories, libraries, and good athletic facilities cost a lot of money. But the fact is that much of the money spent by Alaska schools goes for the transportation of small numbers of students over very long distances, because there are too few students to justify neighborhood schools. In addition, because there are not enough students in Alaska to set up specialized courses, the state flies some of its high-school students to boarding schools in Washington and pays their expenses there. And because living costs in Alaska are very high, teachers must be paid high salaries. But since the statistics don't tell you any of this, can you conclude anything about the quality of education in Alaska?

Usually, when people present you with comparative rates, their purpose is to offer you "statistical proof" of certain conclusions they'd like you to draw. Remember that, no matter how accurate they are, rate differences by themselves can never prove anything.

WHAT'S YOUR AVERAGE?

Probably the most common statistical statement you are likely to encounter—not only in your reading and television viewing but also in school and among your friends—contains the word *average*. "The average American family now has 1.3 children." "Your average grade for the semester is . . ." "The average American car has a life of seven years."

Averages are so simple that you probably learned to calculate them in the fifth grade. To figure out, for example, the average amount you spend for lunch during the week, you simply add what you spent on each of the five days and divide the total by five.

The trouble with this kind of average is that it's *too* simple. Obviously you've never met a family that actually had 1.3 children, and, although the average car may last seven years, you probably know someone who has a twelve-year-old car and someone who totaled his car when it was only one month old. To see the problems that averages present, let's look at the school records of two students, both of whom earned an average grade of 80 after taking the same five subjects.

	Student A	*Student B*
SOCIAL STUDIES	85	75
ALGEBRA	92	75
ENGLISH	83	75
GENERAL SCIENCE	84	75
SPANISH	56	100
Average	80	80

Each of these students had the same average but, on the basis of the grades that make up this average, would you regard them as similar students? Which one do you think would be more successful in college?

This kind of average, called the *mean,* is frequently used because it is so easy to calculate, but it can often mislead you more seriously than it did with respect to Students A and B. Suppose, for example, a small business firm has two partners, each of whom earns $40,000 a year, and nine workers, each of whom earns $12,000 a year. One of the partners may remark that "the average salary in our firm is about $17,000 a year"—yet it's obvious that nobody in the firm earns anything close to this figure. Whenever you see a figure that's described as an "average," the chances are that it's a mean—and therefore possibly quite meaningless.

Competent scientists and statisticians, who are fully aware of the limitations of the mean, often prefer to use two other kinds of average that give a clearer picture of reality. These are called the *median* and the *mode.*

To calculate the *median,* a statistician ranks all the numbers he is working with in order of size. He then counts them and selects the one in the middle of the ranking. This median number often shows a more accurate picture of the situation than the mean does, even though the mean is mathematically more exact. For Students A and B, for instance, the median grades (as you can figure out for yourself) would be 84 and 75 respectively—and these figures show up differences between these students that were concealed by the "average" or mean.

Medians are often used for statistics about incomes because they give a more realistic figure. A mean income figure for the American family would be unrealistically low because there are significant numbers of families (on welfare) who earn nothing at all. The median, on the other hand, represents the family "in the middle"—midway between the very poorest and the very richest.

The third type of average, the *mode,* is also useful because it describes certain situations more accurately than the other types. The mode is simply the most frequently occurring figure in the set of numbers that you're dealing with. Suppose, for example, your daily school lunch costs for a week were 65¢, 75¢, $1.50, 75¢, 75¢. The mode would be 75¢, which is a fairly accurate representation because it tells you what you *usually* spend for lunch. The mean (which would be 88¢) gives you an amount that you never did spend.

There are many situations in which the mode is more useful than either the mean or the median. If you are going to the Caribbean for a winter vacation, presumably you'd like to know the daytime temperature at the beach where you intend to swim. A mean daytime temperature of 70°F. tells you very little, because it could represent a temperature that varies only between 69° and 71°F. or one that varies between 55° and 85°F. But if you find out that the *modal* temperature is 71°F., you would feel confident that the temperature was 71° *more often than any other reading,* because that is what a mode represents.

Competent statisticians almost always indicate whether they are giving you a mean, a median, or a mode—and the fact that they do this should persuade you that they are using the most appropriate of the three. But when nothing is specified, be suspicious. The probability is that you are looking at a mean, which was chosen either deliberately to mislead you or because the person calculating it didn't know any better—in which case you may be equally misled.

ARE YOU "AVERAGE"?

A New Jersey high-school principal, asked why he refused to administer national achievement tests to his students, explained, "On all those tests, about half my students came out below average." His comment expresses a misunderstanding of averages that is widespread. The fact is, of course, that since an average is computed by combining high scores with low scores, about half of any population *must* fall below the average to balance the half that falls above it.

But what does a below-average or above-average score really mean? On an IQ test (on which the average is, by definition, 100), does your score of 105 mean that you're bright—or a score of 95 mean that you're dumb? We can answer this question by shifting our attention from the various kinds of average—all of which are expressed in a single number—to the actual information that goes to make up the average. Once you see what this information "looks like," you will have a much clearer understanding not only about your IQ score but about all sorts of averages.

Let's begin by supposing that you are the proprietor of a shoe store which, being near a large high school, is patronized heavily by young women aged twelve through eighteen. Obviously, you are interested in stocking the sizes that are most likely to fit these customers, and you don't want to waste space on sizes too large or too small. You could, of course, add up the individual sizes of, say, 200 of these young women, divide the total by 200 and arrive at the average (mean) size. But discovering that the average size was, for example, seven would hardly tell you the *range* of sizes you'd need to stock.

But if, instead of calculating the average mathematically, you were to tally up the actual sizes worn by each of the 200 young women, your 200 tally marks would look something like this:

```
                              x
                              x
                      x       x       x
                      x       x       x
                      x       x       x
              x       x       x       x       x
              x       x       x       x       x
              x       x       x       x       x
              x       x       x       x       x
              x       x       x       x       x
      x       x       x       x       x       x       x
      x       x       x       x       x       x       x
      x       x       x       x       x       x       x
      x       x       x       x       x       x       x
      x       x       x       x       x       x       x
      x       x       x       x       x       x       x
  x   x       x       x       x       x       x       x   x
  x   x       x       x       x       x       x       x   x
  x   x       x       x       x       x       x       x   x
  x   x       x       x       x       x       x       x   x
  x   x       x       x       x       x       x       x   x
x x   x       x       x       x       x       x       x   x
x x   x       x       x       x       x       x       x   x   x
x x x x x x x x x x x x x x x x x x x x x x x x x x   x   x   x
x x x x x x x x x x x x x x x x x x x x x x x x x x x x x x   x
x x x x x x x x x x x x x x x x x x x x x x x x x x x x x x x x
  —   —   —   —   —   —   —   —   —   —   —   —   —   —   —
 −4   4  4½   5  5½   6  6½   7  7½   8  8½   9  9½  10 10+
```

This is the size distribution that the shoe-store proprietor found after surveying 200 customers.

Now, if you were to draw a line joining these scores, you would get a curve that represents one of the most important ideas in statistics. It's called a *normal distribution curve*, it is always bell-shaped, and it always results when any one of a vast number of characteristics—not only shoe size but IQ scores, the height of twelve-year-old girls, the number of hours per week that high-school freshmen spend on home-work, and countless others—is plotted *for a large number of people.* (If you try to plot such a curve for fifteen or twenty of your classmates—using, for example, the number of hours per week that they spend watching television—you probably won't get a perfectly symmetrical bell shape because, as we've noted, a perfect curve requires more than fifteen or twenty pieces of information, but your curve will probably be *roughly* bell-shaped.)

What this curve tells us is that, although not everybody wears a size seven, more people wear that size than any other. In addition, the most widely worn sizes cluster close to seven, and the farther we move away from the center in either direction, the fewer the people needing those sizes. From this curve the shoe-store proprietor can see that if he carries only size seven (the average), he'll disappoint a great many customers, but that he can safely carry fewer size tens than size eights, because fewer customers will ask for them.

IQ scores follow the same pattern. Although more students score 100 than any other score, more scores fall in the range between 90 and 110 than anywhere else. And scores become less frequent toward each end of the curve.

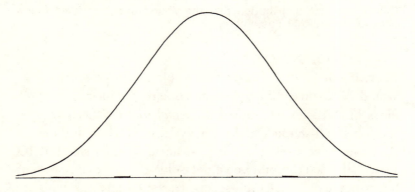

All normal distribution curves are symmetrical and bell-shaped.

By using a mathematical formula, statisticians can calculate for any set of numbers a "distance" along the horizontal axis called the *standard deviation.* On any normal distribution curve, about 68 percent of cases (that is, shoe sizes or IQ scores or anything else) fall within one standard deviation on either side of the center, 95 percent fall within two standard deviations in both directions, and 99.7 percent fall within three. On IQ tests, the standard deviation is ten. This means that more than two-thirds of all students taking the test fall within this range—and this is why any score between 90 and 110 is regarded not as bright or dumb but as normal.

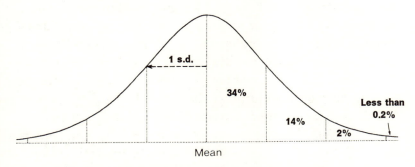

Mean

The standard deviation tells you the range within which *most* (68 percent) of the numbers fall. Note how rapidly the numbers fall off beyond each successive standard deviation.

But what if your IQ score is 122 or 145? A score of 122 lies more than *two* standard deviations beyond the midpoint, and these scores are made by only one out of twenty students. And a score of 145 lies beyond *three* standard deviations, where only three out of a thousand scores occur. If you take IQs seriously, either of these scores indicate you're pretty bright.

As you can now see, a one-number average is almost mean-

ingless unless you also know the standard deviation. Two
cities, for example, may have the same July mean temperature of 78°F. But if one has a standard deviation of 4°, which
means that 68 percent of all readings fall between 74° and
82°, and the other has a standard deviation of 15° (68 percent fall between 63° and 93°), the two cities have very
different climates—a fact that a simple average won't tell
you. As you can see, the larger the standard deviation, the
less meaningful the average.

If you make the normal distribution curve an integral part
of your thinking, you'll find it a splendid device for distin-
guishing between what is *typical* and what is *possible*. If, for
example, you read or hear that a high school dropout is now
earning $150,000 a year as president of a corporation, think
about a normal distribution curve of the earnings of high
school dropouts or a curve of the educational levels of corporation executives. You're likely to conclude, quite correctly,
that the dropout would be at the far end of either curve—
that is, that his situation is possible but certainly not typical.

The normal distribution curve can also help you understand another important point. Because every such curve is
based on *characteristics* of people—heights, weights, IQ
scores, etc.—and not on the people themselves, such phrases
as "the average family" or "the average person" are meaningless. The person who is average in height or weight may be
far from average in income, education, size of house, number
of children, or any of the thousands of other characteristics
that could be plotted on a normal distribution curve. No
individual or family is average in all respects, and anyone
who uses the term "average" so broadly either doesn't understand it or is trying to put something over on you.

IS "AVERAGE" GOOD OR BAD?

Because you are a student, you probably think, like the New Jersey high-school principal, that being "below average" is a bad thing. In fact, you may feel unhappy or insulted if somebody calls you an "average student." But it's very important to keep in mind that an average is simply a mathematical expression and not, in itself, a measure of your virtues or failings.

Although you may feel bad when your grades are below average, you should feel good about being average in blood pressure or heart rate—or shoe size, because you'll have a wider variety from which to choose. And being below average in the number of traffic tickets people your age receive is not a bad thing either.

IS THE BOTTLE HALF FULL
OR HALF EMPTY?

If two people look at a quart bottle containing exactly one pint of water, one of them may describe it as "half full" and the other may describe it as "half empty." Both are equally correct in drawing different conclusions from the same statistic. This example has often been used to describe the difference between an optimist and a pessimist, but it also illustrates an important point about your use of statistics.

Reliable statistics can help you to understand situations accurately (and sometimes to make predictions). They don't, however, hand you ready-made conclusions. To reach conclusions, you must rely to some extent on your judgment.

For this reason, when you see a statistic, think about the reverse of whatever it tells you. If an opinion poll tells you that "53 percent of Americans approve of the president's foreign policy," bear in mind that 47 percent either disapprove or haven't thought about it and that, although 53 percent is technically a majority, it hardly reflects a strongly united nation. If you read that unemployment stands at 9 percent, you can also see that 91 percent of the people who want jobs have them. Whether you feel that a 9-percent rate of unemployment is outrageous or acceptable has nothing to do with statistics. All statistics can ever do is describe reality.

YOU'D BETTER BELIEVE IT!

In this chapter we've pointed out so many of the flaws and limitations of statistics that you may possibly conclude that you ought to distrust *all* statistics. This would be a serious mistake. Although they can be misused by ignorant people and by people with an axe to grind, statistics remain the most useful tool of scientists and one of the most efficient devices you can use to learn about the real world. Knowing the ways in which statistics can be misused can help you use them more effectively to educate yourself and to present your own views convincingly.

As we saw in Chapter 2, no matter how keenly interested we are in what goes on in the world, we can't, as individuals, see anything "as a whole," because our personal observations are always limited or colored by our prejudices, by the narrowness of our experience, by our neighborhood, by the people we know, and by what we've been taught. Statistics, on the other hand, if they have been gathered from reliable sources and put together by honest and well-trained professionals, can tell us about realities that we can't possibly discover for ourselves.

You can prove this point for yourself by asking your friends, your parents, and their friends some of the following questions:

Do women working at the same jobs as men earn the same pay?

Are black babies born in the United States today likely to live as long as white babies?

Are Americans drinking less liquor or smoking fewer cigarettes than they did five years ago?

How tall are the average American man and woman?

Which city has the larger population, Detroit or Pittsburgh?

Compare the answers you get with the answers you can find in *Statistical Abstract of the United States* or in some other source in your public library. If you offer the statistical answers to the people you've questioned, you may find that some of them get a bit annoyed with you (or with themselves). But you're unlikely to find anyone who will argue, "The statistics are wrong and I'm right!"

7

Can Statistics Protect You from Man-eating Tigers?

"Why do you have goose grease all over your face?"
"It protects me from man-eating tigers."
"But there isn't a tiger for miles around."
"It works, doesn't it?"

Reliable statistics, as we've just seen, can offer us an accurate description of a situation or event. If, for example, you look up the U.S. Bureau of the Census figures on the median household income, you'll probably realize that most American families earn less than you thought they did. If you read the government figures on average monthly temperatures in Raleigh, North Carolina, and Detroit, Michigan, you'll note that winters in North Carolina are somewhat warmer than in Michigan—but possibly not as much warmer as you thought. In short, good statistics can make many of our ideas and notions correspond more closely to reality.

But statistics can do more than describe a situation. If we use them carefully, they can also help us to *predict* the future and—even more important—to *explain* or *understand* what goes on around us. But predicting or explaining through the use of statistics is a very tricky and difficult process. On the one hand, good statistics give us confidence that we are dealing with "what's really out there." On the other hand, statistics in themselves, no matter how reliable, can't protect us against jumping to wrong conclusions, whether we are trying to predict next summer's weather or to explain *why* students whose parents are well-to-do earn higher SAT scores than students whose parents are poor.

And so, when someone presents you with a prediction or an explanation based on "statistical evidence," you can't assume that it is valid simply because the statistics seem reliable. Instead, you need to ask yourself whether the prediction or explanation has avoided the pitfalls and errors described in this chapter.

"ALL OTHER THINGS BEING EQUAL"

If we have statistics covering several years in the past and if these statistics don't show much change from year to year, it is often possible to make predictions for future years. If, for example, you know that every year for the past ten years somewhere between 45,000 and 50,000 Americans are killed in automobile accidents, you can predict very confidently that next year's figures will not be as low as 2,000 or as high as 100,000. If you look at summer temperatures for New York City, you can be quite certain that you needn't take along your down jacket when you visit New York next July. If the U.S. Bureau of the Census tells you that, over the past five years, approximately 3.5 million children were born annually, you can be sure that next year this figure will not plunge to 1 million or jump to 7 million. We can make such predictions safely because most conditions or events or behaviors don't change dramatically from one year to the next.

But can we predict next year's traffic fatalities or New York summer temperatures more closely than we've just done? Can we predict that next year 48,970 people will die in accidents, or that the New York temperature on July 14 will be 91°F., or that 3,473,041 children will be born? Two problems make this kind of prediction impossible.

First, prediction about an event can be accurate only if all conditions influencing the event remain unchanged. (This is what is meant by the stock phrase "all other things being equal.") Unfortunately, "all other things" don't always remain unchanged. Any prediction about traffic fatalities may be changed, for example, by an unexpected gasoline shortage, by laws requiring air bags or the wearing of seatbelts—or by an economic slump. (For reasons nobody understands, the fatality rate always drops when times are bad.)

A few years ago, the birth rate dropped sharply and unexpectedly (and wrecked the predictions of school planners and the manufacturers of diapers and baby foods, among others) apparently because the newly developed birth-control pill proved much more popular than anyone had anticipated. On the other hand, right now the birth rate is climbing for the first time in years—for reasons that nobody has been able to pinpoint. Even the summer temperature in New York next July may reach a "record high" or a "record low" because of changes in the jet stream, air pollution, or some other condition, known or unknown.

Second, even when all other things *are* equal most events normally show what is called a "statistical fluctuation"—that is, a small change in the figures from year to year that occurs simply by chance. For example, statisticians can't explain why in 1978 105.3 boys were born for every 100 girls, while in 1979 the boy-girl ratio was 105.2 to 100—but they don't really care. Even though the difference amounts to about 3,000 children, it is so small in relation to the large total numbers involved that they dismiss it as "normal."

But when total numbers are small, these normal fluctuations can produce inaccurate or dishonest predictions. If in your town, for example, there were four murders last year but only two this year, the newspaper headline ————'s HOMICIDE RATE DROPPING SHARPLY is absurd. True, the difference of two murders represents a 50-percent reduction, but a difference of only two murders is so likely to be caused by chance that it can't be interpreted as a long-term trend.

Both normal statistical fluctuation and unanticipated changes in "other things" make accurate prediction very difficult. But many people, through either ignorance or dishonesty, overlook these difficulties and make faulty predictions. Worse yet, as we shall see shortly, they make serious errors in understanding or explaining events.

RELATIONSHIPS—MEANINGFUL AND OTHERWISE

In addition to prediction, statistics can be used to help us discover that two phenomena which at first glance appear to have nothing to do with each other are, in fact, related in a systematic way. For example, if we look at SAT scores and the educational level of each student's parents, we find that the high scorers on the SAT tend to have well-educated parents and the low scorers have parents with less education. Or, to cite another example, when we check the grade records of college students against the records of their participation in collegiate athletics, we find that students who are not members of the college teams consistently earn higher grades than the jocks.

Such relationships between two sets of statistics are called "correlations" or "covariance," because the two sets (let's call them *A* and *B*) have a systematic relationship with each other—that is, they vary together. In the case of SAT scores and parents' education, the correlation is *positive*, because when A is high, B is high, and when A is low, B is low; in the case of college grades and athletic participation, the correlation is *negative*, because when A is high, B is low, and when A is low, B is high.

Actually, it makes no difference whether a correlation is positive or negative. As long as it is strong and consistent, we may be able to find out *why* or *how* A and B are related and thus learn something about either or both of them. In fact, a great deal of scientific work consists in looking for new correlations or trying to explain those that have been discovered.

It's important to note that no correlation is perfect. There will always be some exceptions: high SAT scorers from poor or uneducated families, or star quarterbacks who make the honor roll. But when a correlation is strong, these exceptions are few. For example, the correlation (positive) between people's weight and their height is rather strong: most tall people weigh more than most short people, even though we all know some short roly-polies and some skinny six-footers.

But most correlations are more interesting and less obvious than the one between height and weight, and many of them challenge or change our ideas. For example, despite all the detective stories you may have read, your chances of being murdered are strongly and negatively correlated with your parents' income: the higher their income, the lower your chances. And the likelihood of your being executed for homicide is more strongly (and negatively) correlated with your income, education, and race than it is with your actual guilt —or with the jury's verdict. To cite a more likely example, if you are male, your chances of being promoted to the presidency of an organization are more strongly correlated with your height than with your record of achievement.

PREDICTING AND EXPLAINING

Can correlations be used to make predictions? If the correlation is consistent over a period of years, and if all other things remain equal, the answer is a strong yes.

College admissions officers, for example, who use your SAT score in their decision to admit you do so because there is a positive correlation between SAT performance and the grades a student achieves in college. (The correlation is not very strong, but using it in addition to your high-school record, they feel, is far sounder than admitting you on the basis of your looks or on sheer hunch.) College athletics departments set up permanent academic coaching sessions for their star athletes because they predict that next year's athletes will earn no better grades than last year's. City planners who decide to situate a new hospital in the slums rather than the affluent suburbs base their decision on the strong negative correlation between family income and the likelihood of being injured or becoming ill. Bear in mind, though, that all of these predictions are based on correlations that will remain strong only if all other things remain equal.

But can correlations, even when they are strong and stable enough to be used for prediction, be used for understanding or explanation—that is, do they tell us what *causes* an event? As we noted in Chapter 5, it is all too easy to jump to questionable conclusions about causation. But statistical relationships, simply because they involve reliable numbers, make jumping to such conclusions even easier. When we encounter a strong correlation—that is, when *A* and *B* are very strongly correlated—can we conclude that *A* is the *cause* of *B*? This is a very difficult question, because the same correlation would exist if *A* caused *B*, if *B* caused *A*, or if something we were not aware of (let's call it C) caused both A and B.

Sometimes we can be fairly certain that A causes B. In some countries, for example, there is a strong correlation between the amount of annual rainfall in an area (A) and the number of cattle raised in that area (B). Here we can safely conclude that A is a cause of B because we know (1) that cattle are even less able to cause rainfall than Navaho rain dancers, (2) that rainfall causes grass to grow, and (3) that grass is good, inexpensive feed for cattle. Since we know also that the rainfall existed earlier in time than cattle raising, we can be fairly certain that it encouraged the cattle raising rather than the other way around.

But very often, when A and B are correlated, there is the possibility that either one causes the other or that both act as causes. The strong negative correlation between mental illness (A) and income (B), for example, may occur because mental illness prevents a person from getting or holding a steady job (A causes B) or because the stresses of poverty are likely to make poor people mentally ill (B causes A) or because "both of the above are true." All three explanations are plausible, but the correlation by itself can't prove that any one of them is correct.

In Japan some years ago, a strong positive correlation was discovered between the number of television sets sold per year (A) and the number of heart attacks (B). Each year, as the sale of television sets increased, so did the number of heart attacks. Given this correlation, what would you say causes it? Does A cause B—that is, is the quality of Japanese television programs so terrible that it produces heart attacks in the viewers? (Actually, it's neither better nor worse than what we see in the United States.) Or does B cause A—that is, are more people suffering heart attacks and being told by their physicians to relax by buying a television set and sitting in front of it? Or is it possible that the seemingly related increases in both *A* and *B* are caused by some third factor (*C*), which we haven't thought of? Most experts on the subject think they have identified *C*—the growing economic prosperity in Japan which (1) enabled more people to afford television sets and (2) allowed them a richer diet and a more sedentary life, both of which may contribute to heart attacks.

But, you may ask, if correlation between *A* and *B* tells us nothing about causation, how could we say, a few paragraphs above, that a strong, long-term correlation can be used for prediction? In order to predict a phenomenon, don't we need to understand what causes it? Not necessarily. The ancient Greeks were able to predict the tides by correlating the height of each tide with the phase of the moon. It was not until centuries later that scientists understood that the *cause* of the tide was the gravitational attraction of the moon, but the Greeks, who knew nothing about gravitation, were able to make good predictions by observing consistent correlations over a long period of time. Their predictions would have been correct even if they thought that the tides caused the phases of the moon.

The ancient Romans were also able to make good predictions without understanding causation. They suffered from a disease which they named *malaria*, because they thought it was caused by the "bad air" that emanated from the swamps of Rome, especially during the summer months. To avoid this bad air, they retreated, during the summer, to the surrounding hills—thus originating the summer vacation. And they discovered that going off to the hills did, in fact, protect them against malaria—even though malaria was not, in fact, caused by bad air. Centuries later, the "cause" of malaria was identified as the mosquitoes that bred freely in swampy areas.

Mosquito-eradication programs were undertaken to prevent malaria and, like the Romans' summer vacations, they, too, were effective. Decades later, the "cause" of malaria was identified—this time correctly—as a microorganism that is carried by the anopheles mosquito. But centuries earlier, long before the real cause was identified, preventive programs worked on the basis of correlation.

Today, the correlation between cigarette smoking and lung cancer or heart attacks is so strong that the Surgeon General is justified in placing a warning on all cigarette packages. But the American Tobacco Institute, a lobbying group for the industry, is absolutely right in arguing that there is no scientific evidence that smoking *causes* cancer. Yet, when a correlation is as strong as this one, causation is likely to be lurking somewhere in the relationship, even though today we know as little about the biochemistry of lung cancer as the Greeks knew about the moon's gravitational field or the Romans knew about the anopheles mosquito.

The fact is that if you have ever taken aspirin, you have done so on the basis of correlation and not causation. That is, you are aware that there is a strong relationship between the taking of aspirin and the disappearance of certain unpleasant symptoms. But although aspirin is many decades old and is used by millions of people, even today nobody knows precisely how it works. It was discovered by accident and, although a few people get negative reactions to it, physicians recommend it on the basis of statistics, not an understanding of its biochemistry. To put it simply, aspirin "works"—even though nobody knows why or how.

THE DANGERS OF "BECAUSE"

Although a correlation in itself explains nothing, you'll find it used commonly by politicians, editors, advertisers, and others as evidence supporting their point of view. Politicians, for example, often use statistical relationships to promote their party's interests. Their claim that the inflation rate (or the level of unemployment) dropped immediately after President X took office may be true, but their conclusion that the drop was *caused* by his administration's policies may be (and probably is) nonsense. When the *Wall Street Journal* advertises the fact that its readers earn above-average incomes, it would like you to believe that reading the *Journal* will increase your income. But it is at least as logical to conclude that people with above-average incomes subscribe to the *Journal* because it provides information about investments that are of interest to them.

It's easy enough to see the motives of politicians and advertisers who misinterpret statistical relationships to their own advantage. But many people who have no intention of misleading others interpret statistics only in terms of their personal beliefs, failing to see that the same statistics can lead to very different conclusions.

If, for example, you're convinced that "all jocks are dumb," you can point to the fact that they tend to get low grades. But if you assume that jocks are no more stupid or bright than other students, their poorer academic work can be explained on the grounds that ambitious coaches require them to practice so hard and so long that they have neither the time nor the energy needed for good academic work. This, by the way, is the conclusion of most people who have studied this issue carefully instead of using the correlation to support their preconceived notions.

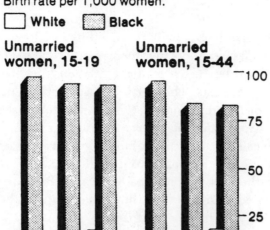

Out-of-Wedlock Births

Birth rate per 1,000 women.

☐ White   ▨ Black

Unmarried women, 15-19   **Unmarried women, 15-44**

100

75

50

25

0

1970 1975 1980   1970 1975 1980

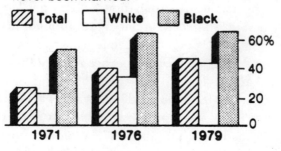

Teen-Agers Who Say They Have Had Intercourse

Percentage, ages 15-19, who have never been married.

▨ Total   ☐ White   ▨ Black

60%

40

20

0

1971   1976   1979

People who believe that the poor are naturally stupid and lazy and that the well-to-do are naturally bright and ambitious will interpret the positive correlation between parents' income and school grades as proof for their position. But the same correlation can be used to support the view that poor neighborhoods have poor schools, poor teachers, and poor libraries, or that poor parents, because they have less education, are less able to help their children with their homework, or that "all of the above are true."

Even when we are not influenced by our beliefs, we may misinterpret a statistical relationship simply because we overlook the fact that all other conditions are *not* equal. When, for example, in order to conserve gasoline and diesel fuel, the national speed limit was lowered to 55 mph, the number of highway fatalities dropped sharply. Many people

---

No matter how detailed and accurate, *descriptive* statistics don't *explain* themselves. The information shown here is reliable as *fact*, but facts alone offer us no clue to the reasons behind them. Readers who are prejudiced against blacks are likely to attribute the differences in the illegitimacy rate to "loose morals," but more objective and more sophisticated readers would raise questions such as the following: "Are there differences in income (and therefore education) between the black and white teenagers?" [Yes. More than three times as many blacks as whites live below the poverty level.] "Do poor teenagers have less knowledge about the access to contraception, adoption, and abortion?" [Yes, and this is supported by the fact that the black-white difference in illegitimate births is much greater than the difference in intercourse.] "Does the welfare system tend to encourage the birth of illegitimate children?" [Possibly, because the young teenager living with her family can qualify for both welfare and Medicaid if she has a baby.] "Does a poor family feel less 'shame' than a well-to-do family when their teenager has an illegitimate baby?" [Yes, according to social scientists.] To sum up, the differences are more likely due to poverty than to "loose morals." Perhaps more important, the *overwhelming majority* of teenagers, black or white, do *not* have illegitimate children.

concluded that the drop was caused by the lowered speed limit. But the same fuel shortage that prompted the lowering of the speed limit also caused many people to drive less, and this lower mileage was further reduced by an economic slump. A reduction in mileage driven will, of course, inevitably reduce the number of accidents, whether or not the speed limit is reduced. And, in fact, as soon as the fuel supply and economic conditions improved, the fatality rate began rising, even though the same speed limit is still in effect. When all these "other conditions" are taken into account, scientists conclude that the reduction in the speed limit has had *some* effect on the fatality rate but not nearly as much as most people believed.

We can sum all this up in two simple rules:

Statistical predictions are likely to be accurate if "all other things are equal." This is why eclipses and tides can be predicted accurately; weather predictions are less accurate because meteorologists can't measure all the "other things" that affect tomorrow's weather. Because predictions about human affairs involve even more "other things," nobody can pinpoint exactly such important events as an economic slump or a change in the rate of inflation. And so, when you are presented with a prediction, ask yourself about the "other things" that may wreck it. The chances are that you'll find a number of them.

Statistics alone can't tell us about causation. When you are offered an explanation of *why* two sets of statistics are related, try to find *other* explanations that would account for the relationship equally well. But remember that an understanding of causation isn't always necessary for prediction. Nobody knows how the universe came into existence, but you can be quite certain that the sun will rise tomorrow.

8

What Are My Chances?

*"You've got to kiss an awful lot of frogs
before you find a prince."*
—*Source unknown*

Benjamin Franklin once said, "In this life, nothing is certain save death and taxes." Scientists would take this statement one step further. No future event, they say, can be predicted with absolute certainty. The fact that the sun has risen in the east and set in the west for as long as humankind has noticed it doesn't guarantee that it will do this tomorrow. (Some totally unforeseen astronomical occurrence may throw the earth out of orbit.) The fact that nobody has managed to swim across the Atlantic Ocean or live to the age of 200 doesn't mean that nobody will ever manage to do it.

But if nothing is predictable—if, in fact, "anything can happen"—does it make any sense for us to plan for the future? Why bother to set your alarm clock tonight, since it may fail to go off tomorrow, or the school bus may not show up, or a meteorite may crash through the roof of your house (as it did not long ago in Connecticut) and kill you?

Yet the fact is that we do make plans for the future, because we can be "quite sure"—even if not absolutely positive—that certain events will (or won't) take place. You can be quite sure, for example, that your alarm clock *will* go off (even though "My alarm didn't work" remains a favorite excuse of tardy students). And you can be even more certain that tomorrow's routine will not be disrupted by a falling meteorite. In short, you can make plans because your common sense and your past experience tell you that some future events have high probability and some are highly *im*probable. If you didn't know this, you could not make any sorts of long-range plans—or even decide on what you'll do tomorrow.

But between the very strong likelihood of tomorrow's sunrise and the almost equally strong unlikelihood that a grizzly bear will invade your bedroom and eat you tonight lie a wide range of probabilities, some high, some moderate, some low. And many of these may govern events that are of some importance to you. For example:

> What are your chances of being killed in an automobile accident within the next ten years?
> If you hope to be a doctor, what are your chances of being admitted to medical school?
> What are the chances that the two children you hope to have will both be girls, even though you'd like to have one boy and one girl—or that one of them will be retarded?
> Is a church raffle ticket or a state lottery ticket a good investment?

Knowing the probabilities here can help you make better decisions than simply going ahead with plans without asking, "What are my chances?"

Is probability just another way of saying "luck"? Not really. Luck is a subjective, personal feeling—that is, people *feel* lucky or unlucky. Probability, on the other hand, is objective, impersonal, and mathematical: it tells us whether our feeling is justified and thus allows us to change our plans. Everyone who buys a lottery ticket, for example, feels lucky; otherwise he wouldn't buy a ticket. But an understanding of probability might convince the ticket buyer that he is far more likely to lose than to win—no matter how often he buys a ticket or how many tickets he buys. To cite another example, if a genetics counselor who has carefully examined the cells of a married couple advises them that their chances of having a retarded child are one in four, the couple, feeling "lucky," might go ahead and have a child but, if they feel that the one-in-four risk is too high, they might adopt one instead.

Luck in itself is rarely responsible for what happens to you. Some events—such as winning a lottery—are, of course, determined entirely by chance (if the lottery is run honestly). But most of your activities that seem to be "strictly a matter of luck" are, in fact, at least partly influenced by your own behavior. If you are a skillful card player, for example, you can often win the game even though, strictly by chance, you were dealt a "lousy" hand. And, although your grade on an exam depends somewhat on chance (on whether the teacher chooses questions you can answer), you can improve the probability of a good grade if you study hard instead of simply writing the exam with your "lucky" pen. Even being struck by lightning or killed by a tornado depends to some extent on whether you paid attention to the weather forecasts.

MATHEMATICAL PROBABILITY

The probability that an event will occur can be calculated by a formula that may strike you as complicated at first glance but that will become simple once we apply it to some examples:

$$\frac{\text{number of occurrences of form A of an outcome}}{\text{number of occurrences of form A} + \text{all other possible forms of outcome}}$$

Let's look at this formula in terms of coin tossing and suppose that we choose heads as form A. If we disregard the very remote possibility that a tossed coin will land on its edge, there is only one "other possible form" of the outcome: tails. And so our formula translates into

$$\frac{\text{heads}}{\text{heads} + \text{tails}} = \frac{1}{2} = 50\text{-percent probability.}$$

If we apply the same formula to a one-prize lottery, with the winning ticket designated as form A, your probability of winning can be calculated as

$$\frac{1 \text{ (your ticket)}}{1 \text{ (your ticket)} + \text{all the other tickets sold}}$$

But, although these formulas are simple, both coin tossing and lottery winning are a bit more complicated, and we'll come back to them later on.

As long as we know the number of occurrences of form A and the number of occurrences of "all other possible forms," we can calculate probability simply by applying our formula. And so, for example, knowing that each of a pair of dice has six sides, we can say that the probability that the number we want will come up on one of them is 1 in 6—provided the dice aren't "loaded." The same formula can be applied to your combination lock. If yours is typical, with thirty numbers on the dial and three numbers in the combination, your probability of guessing the right combination (form A) in one trial is about 1 in 27,000.

An understanding of probability can help you decide whether or not to buy a raffle or a lottery ticket. Let's suppose your church or your local PTA holds a raffle for a $6,000 car, with tickets offered at a dollar each. At the point at which 6,000 tickets have been sold, the sponsor has broken even (unless, of course, someone donated the car). But the purpose of such a raffle is not to break even but to make money, and hence many more than 6,000 tickets are likely to be sold. Suppose you've bought one of the 8,500 tickets that eventually get sold. You now have a 1-in-8,500 probability of winning, but if you do win, your prize is worth only 6,000 times your original one-dollar investment. That is, your odds of winning are less than your odds of losing. Obviously there is no way in which you could come out ahead. Would buying two tickets improve your chances? Two tickets would give you a 1-in-4,250 probability of winning, but your win would now be 3,000 to 1. Is a raffle ticket worth buying? Yes if you're feeling charitable, no if you expect to come out ahead.

A state lottery ticket offers you the same unfavorable odds. Bear in mind that before paying out prize money, the state deducts perhaps 20 percent of the money it gets from ticket sales for operating expenses and for the support of schools, hospitals, and other state-financed activities. And so, because the available prize money has been reduced, your payoff will be 80 percent of what the actual probability indicates it should be. If the state were to pay out on the basis of the mathematical probability, it would lose money—that is, the costs of running the lottery. This same tactic of paying out less than probability dictates accounts for the prosperity of the gambling casinos in Las Vegas and Atlantic City. Whether at cards, dice, slot machines, or the roulette wheel, the odds are calculated so that "the house" has a small but consistent advantage—usually no more than 2 percent. This is why, although many people make lucky wins, it's impossible for a gambler to come out ahead over the long term.

When probabilities are easily calculated in advance—as in our examples of coin tossing or lottery tickets—there is nothing you can do to change the outcome for yourself, because, in such situations, what you do or fail to do doesn't count. The coin is not influenced by who tosses it; the lock won't yield its combination more readily to one person than to another; and the official drawing the winning lottery ticket doesn't know who bought it.

But knowing their mathematical probability can help you deal with some situations more intelligently. Once you understand that you have only a 1-in-27,000 chance of guessing the combination of your lock, you're likely to feel confident that it will protect your locker from thieves—and to memorize the combination and keep a copy in a safe place! Once you know that over the long run in a friendly game of coin tossing you will neither win nor lose, you will either play the game because you think it's fun or abandon it as a waste of time, but you won't play it in the hope of winning a lot of money. Once a woman understands that she has a 1-in-4 chance of having a retarded child, she can base her choice on scientific fact, not on wild optimism or bleak pessimism.

These probabilities, based on mathematics and logic, are completely trustworthy *over the long run*. This means that if you gamble at Las Vegas long enough, you will lose about 2 percent of your money or that if you have a great many children, half of them are likely to be boys and half girls. But over the short run the laws of probability don't seem to work quite so precisely. Although the chances are 50 percent that a tossed coin will land heads, you may, in some games, get a consecutive run of ten or more tails. This is why many gamblers at Las Vegas win big or have a lucky streak in one evening's play, but they are certain to give their winnings back if they play long enough to let the laws of probability take effect. And although the probability of having a boy baby rather than a girl is just about 50 percent (not quite, because about 105 boys are born for each 100 girls), you may know of families consisting of four or five daughters because the parents kept on having children in the hope of having a son. It's even possible (though *very* improbable) that a thief will guess the combination of your lock on his first try.

PROBABILITY BY EXPERIENCE

Thus far we've discussed calculating the probability of an event by the use of logic and mathematics. But it is also possible (though much more difficult) to calculate probabilities when we don't know in advance the precise numbers for A and non-A. Suppose, for example, that the U.S. Bureau of the Census would like to know the life expectancy of the American population—that is, whether you are more likely to die at age sixty-five or at age eighty. Or suppose that insurance companies would like to calculate the probability that you will have an automobile accident. Or suppose that Harvard University would like to know what an applicant's chances are of being admitted.

When we use our probability formula for life expectancy, A is the number of deaths each year that occur at a specified age—say, age seventy-two—and non-A is the total number of deaths at all ages that occurred during the same year. For accident probability, A is the number of drivers who report accidents and non-A is the total number of licensed drivers. For Harvard admission, A is the number of candidates admitted and non-A is the number applying. In all these examples, the calculation is based on actual experience: on the number of deaths reported to public-health authorities, on the number of accidents reported to the police, or on the number of applications for admission to Harvard.

GROWTH OF THE AMERICAN LIFE SPAN

YEAR	LIFE SPAN (in yrs.)	YEAR	LIFE SPAN (in yrs.)	YEAR	LIFE SPAN (in yrs.)	YEAR	LIFE SPAN (in yrs.)	YEAR	LIFE SPAN (in yrs.)	YEAR	LIFE SPAN (in yrs.)
1900	47.3	1935	61.7	1950	68.2	1962	70.0	1968	70.2	1974	71.9
1910	50.0	1938	63.5	1955	69.6	1963	69.6	1969	70.4	1975	72.5
1915	54.5	1940	62.9	1957	69.5	1964	70.2	1970	70.9	1976	72.8
1920	54.1	1943	63.3	1958	69.6	1965	70.2	1971	71.1	1977	73.2
1925	59.0	1945	65.9	1960	69.7	1966	70.1	1972	71.1	1978	73.3
1930	59.7	1948	67.2	1961	70.2	1967	70.5	1973	71.3	1979	73.8

Source: U.S. Public Health Service

A life-expectancy table of this type tells us that Americans today live longer than they did in the past, but it doesn't tell us much else. Has life expectancy increased because infant mortality has fallen off or because older people are living longer? And what kinds of people are likely to die early in life? The table on pages 128-129 gives us much more information.

You can see immediately why these probabilities are less reliable than those based on mathematics and logic. To begin with, unlike mathematical-logical probabilities, which will be as reliable a century from now as they are today, probabilities based on experience change from year to year. Life expectancy in the United States, for example, has increased by four years during the past twenty years. The automobile accident rate (for reasons nobody understands) tends to drop when times are bad. (And so, incidentally, does the divorce rate.) And the rejection rate at Harvard may change not only with the availability of scholarships but also if Harvard decides to enlarge its student body. If you plan to use such probabilities, you must make certain that they are based on the most recent figures available.

But there are other problems. If such probabilities are based on a whole population—*all* deaths in the case of life expectancy or *all* licensed drivers in the case of automobile accidents, or *all* applicants to Harvard—they include several groups of people whose "experience"—in terms of death or automobile accidents or admission to Harvard—is very different from one another, but these differences won't show up in the overall figures. For example, blacks (for reasons that are only partly understood) have a distinctly lower life expectancy than whites, and women live longer than men. Teenagers (and bartenders!) are more likely to have accidents than their elders (and college professors!). And, other things being equal, prep-school graduates are more likely to get into Harvard than graduates of public high schools.

This is why the U.S. Bureau of the Census constructs separate life-expectancy tables for whites and for "nonwhites," and why automobile insurance companies charge lower premiums for "low-risk" groups, such as middle-aged professionals, than for "high-risk" groups, such as teenaged males and drivers who have been convicted of several traffic violations. But many such experience-based probabilities overlook these refinements. Figures on the divorce rate, for example, may tell you that one in three marriages ends in divorce; but they don't tell you that your probability of divorce will be much higher than this if you marry young, have little education, and don't earn much money. Figures on black life expectancy include newborn babies, who are two to four times more likely than white babies to die before their first birthday, in part because so many of them live in poverty and get poor medical care. These infant deaths, of course, lower black life expectancy sharply. If, then, you are a black adolescent, your life expectancy is likely to be considerably higher than such a table shows—because you have safely passed through the dangerous period of infancy. In fact, the U.S. government regularly publishes tables from which you can determine the life expectancies of whites and nonwhites on each birthday. Such tables show, for example, that a white male aged sixty-five can expect to live another fourteen years.

EXPECTATION OF LIFE IN YEARS

Age	Total persons	White		All other	
		Male	Female	Male	Female
0	73.3	70.2	77.8	65.0	73.6
1	73.3	70.1	77.6	65.5	74.0
2	72.4	69.2	76.7	64.6	73.1
3	71.5	68.3	75.7	63.7	72.1
4	70.5	67.3	74.8	62.8	71.2
5	69.5	66.3	73.8	61.8	70.2
6	68.6	65.4	72.8	60.8	69.3
7	67.6	64.4	71.8	59.9	68.3
8	66.6	63.4	70.8	58.9	67.3
9	65.6	62.4	69.9	57.9	66.3
10	64.6	61.5	68.9	57.0	65.4
11	63.7	60.5	67.9	56.0	64.4
12	62.7	59.5	66.9	55.0	63.4
13	61.7	58.5	65.9	54.0	62.4
14	60.7	57.5	64.9	53.1	61.4
15	59.7	56.6	64.0	52.1	60.4
16	58.8	55.6	63.0	51.1	59.5
17	57.8	54.7	62.0	50.2	58.5
18	56.9	53.8	61.1	49.3	57.5
19	56.0	52.9	60.1	48.3	56.6
20	55.0	52.0	59.1	47.4	55.6
21	54.1	51.1	58.2	46.5	54.7
22	53.2	50.2	57.2	45.7	53.7
23	52.2	49.3	56.2	44.8	52.8
24	51.3	48.4	55.3	43.9	51.8
25	50.4	47.5	54.3	43.1	50.9
26	49.5	46.5	53.3	42.2	49.9
27	48.5	45.6	52.4	41.4	49.0
28	47.6	44.7	51.4	40.5	48.1
29	46.6	43.8	50.4	39.7	47.1
30	45.7	42.8	49.5	38.8	46.2
31	44.8	41.9	48.5	37.9	45.2
32	43.8	41.0	47.5	37.1	44.3
33	42.9	40.0	46.6	36.2	43.4
34	41.9	39.1	45.6	35.4	42.5
35	41.0	38.2	44.6	34.5	41.5
36	40.1	37.2	43.7	33.7	40.6
37	39.1	36.3	42.7	32.9	39.7
38	38.2	35.4	41.8	32.0	38.8
39	37.3	34.5	40.8	31.2	37.9
40	36.4	33.6	39.9	30.4	37.0
41	35.5	32.6	38.9	29.6	36.1
42	34.6	31.7	38.0	28.9	35.3
43	33.7	30.8	37.1	28.1	34.4
44	32.8	29.9	36.1	27.3	33.5
45	31.9	29.1	35.2	26.5	32.7
46	31.0	28.2	34.3	25.8	31.8
47	30.1	27.3	33.4	25.0	31.0
48	29.3	26.5	32.5	24.3	30.2
49	28.4	25.6	31.6	23.5	29.3

Age	Total persons	White		All other	
		Male	Female	Male	Female
50	27.6	24.8	30.7	22.8	28.5
51	26.7	24.0	29.8	22.1	27.8
52	25.9	23.2	29.0	21.4	27.0
53	25.1	22.4	28.1	20.8	26.2
54	24.3	21.6	27.3	20.1	25.5
55	23.5	20.8	26.4	19.5	24.7
56	22.7	20.1	25.6	18.9	24.0
57	22.0	19.3	24.7	18.3	23.3
58	21.2	18.6	23.9	17.7	22.5
59	20.5	17.9	23.1	17.1	21.8
60	19.7	17.2	22.3	16.5	21.2
61	19.0	16.5	21.5	16.0	20.5
62	18.3	15.8	20.7	15.5	19.9
63	17.6	15.2	19.9	15.1	19.3
64	17.0	14.6	19.2	14.6	18.6
65	16.3	14.0	18.4	14.1	18.0
66	15.7	13.4	17.7	13.6	17.3
67	15.0	12.8	16.9	13.1	16.7
68	14.4	12.2	16.2	12.5	16.0
69	13.7	11.6	15.5	12.0	15.4
70	13.1	11.1	14.8	11.6	14.8
71	12.5	10.6	14.1	11.1	14.2
72	12.0	10.1	13.4	10.7	13.7
73	11.4	9.6	12.7	10.4	13.2
74	10.9	9.1	12.1	10.0	12.8
75	10.4	8.6	11.5	9.8	12.5
76	9.9	8.2	10.9	9.5	12.2
77	9.4	7.8	10.3	9.3	11.9
78	9.0	7.4	9.8	9.1	11.7
79	8.5	7.1	9.3	8.9	11.6
80	8.1	6.7	8.8	8.8	11.5
81	7.8	6.4	8.3	8.7	11.3
82	7.4	6.1	7.9	8.6	11.1
83	7.1	5.8	7.5	8.5	10.9
84	6.7	5.5	7.1	8.2	10.5
85	6.4	5.3	6.7	7.8	9.9

Sources: Metropolitan Life Insurance Company; Department of Health and Human Services, National Center for Health Statistics. NOTE: Data are latest available.

Unlike the preceding table, this one gives us a great deal of interesting information—for example, on the higher infant-mortality rates among blacks. But it also raises some questions without answering them. Why, for example, do women of every age outlive men, and why do blacks, who have a shorter life expectancy than whites for most of their lives, begin to outlive them in the later years?

To use probability tables of any kind intelligently, then, you must ask yourself, "Do I differ in any important way from the large population on which the probability is based?" If, for example, you are a black teenager whose parents are middle-class professionals, able to give you good nutrition and medical care, your life expectancy will be closer to the white than to the black. And if you have a nondescript high-school record, mediocre SAT scores, and no compensating virtues, your chances of getting into Harvard are a lot lower than any probability figures may promise, because your qualifications are not as high as those of *most* applicants.

Like mathematical probabilities, experience-based probabilities are most reliable over a long run and with a large population. Your sixty-five-year-old neighbor, Mr. Jones, for whom the table predicts another fourteen years of life, may, in fact, die today, or he may live to age ninety-six. What the table tells him is that *most* men aged sixty-five are likely to die in *approximately* fourteen years, although *some* will die much sooner and *some* much later.

This difference between "most" and "some" is what enables life-insurance companies to calculate their premiums when they sell you a policy. Basically they set their premiums so that they will make a profit if you die at your normal life expectancy. If you die earlier, they will lose money, but this doesn't matter because they will regain this money from people who outlive the normal life expectancy and keep paying premiums. But it's important to realize that insurance companies base their calculations on many thousands of policy holders and not on a single event—and, as we've noted, the accuracy of a probability depends on the number of people or cases involved. The probability that the horse you pick will win an eight-horse race is very much lower. This is why, as one statistician has put it, insurance companies get rich and bettors on horse races get poor.

In a very real sense, every insurance policy is a bet. In return for your premium, the insurance company is betting you that something bad—your death, for example, or an automobile accident—*won't* happen to you. If it does happen, the insurance company pays off; if not, the insurance company has won your premium, you get nothing, and you renew your bet for another year by paying another premium.

Now, if the actual probability (based on the insurance company's long experience with thousands of people your age) that you will die this year is 1 in 10,000, this year's premium for a $5,000 life-insurance policy should cost you only fifty cents. But at this rate the insurance company (like the state lottery we mentioned earlier) would make no money, since it would be paying out exactly what it took in. And so your premium is considerably more than fifty cents and does not reflect the actual probability. To put it in another way, your bet with the insurance company offers you unfavorable odds.

Even if they know that the odds are unfavorable, however, your parents probably buy life insurance because they haven't enough money to provide for you if something should happen to them in the near future. For the same reason, they buy automobile liability insurance, because they could not afford to pay a $200,000 damage claim if they were found to be at fault in a serious accident. But a life-insurance policy on *your* life is a less sensible investment for three good reasons: first, the death rate at your age is extremely low; second, your death won't deprive them of financial support; and, third, money is not going to make them happier if you should die.

Insurance advertising tries, of course, to heighten our

worries about possible disaster by exaggerating the probabilities. But sophisticated people refuse to insure themselves
against losses they can afford to pay out of their own pockets.
Today, for example, when you rent a car you are responsible
for the first $300 worth of damage in the event of an accident.
You can insure yourself against having to pay the $300 by
buying a supplementary policy for about $7 per day. On the
basis of your own driving experience, do you really think
that your chances of having an accident each day are as high
as 1 in 43? To put this in another way, have you, over the
past year, averaged one accident every forty-three days? If
not, are you willing to place a $7 bet in the hope of winning
$300? In this situation, smart people "self-insure"—that is,
they assume the risk themselves instead of paying a premium
that is very much higher than actual probability justifies.

USING PROBABILITIES

As we've seen, probabilities are important to you even if you
don't intend to become a professional gambler. Properly
used, they can help you make decisions about insurance,
about whether or not to have an operation that your doctor
says has a less than 50-percent chance of success, or choosing
a law school from which only 60 percent of the graduates
pass the bar exam. They can even help you decide whether
you can safely plan a picnic for tomorrow. But if you are to
make good decisions, you need to make sure that the figures
are reliable and that you interpret them correctly.

With mathematical probabilities the question of reliability
doesn't arise, but interpretation becomes very important.
Many women who are told that they have a 1-in-4 chance of
having a mentally retarded baby conclude that it is their
fourth baby who will be retarded, and this won't matter,

since they plan to have only one or two. But probability doesn't work this way. Not only may the retarded baby be their first one but, in fact, their first *two* babies may be retarded. But although this is possible, it is not *probable*— and such a mother can proceed with *some* assurance that her first baby is more likely to be normal than retarded.

It's also important to understand that some probabilities stand alone and that others are interdependent. The three-number combination lock with thirty numbers on its face does *not* give you a 1-in-90 (3 × 30) chance of guessing it right; your chances are 1 in 27,000 because guessing the third number right is of no use unless you guessed the first two. On the other hand, the fact that a family already has two daughters does not change the fact that the next baby's chance of being a son is close to 50–50. All the details of probability are far too complex for discussion here, and many of them require more math than you probably know now, but careful thinking can protect you from gross misinterpretations.

Probabilities based on experience—that is, on data collected by government agencies or businesses—are, by their nature, less reliable than mathematical probabilities, and they need to be scrutinized with a good deal of suspicion. Here are some questions you ought to raise before taking them seriously:

How Reliable Is the "Experience" on Which the Probability Is Based?

Life-expectancy probabilities are highly reliable because almost all births and deaths are reported. Automobile-accident and crime probabilities are much less reliable because large numbers of each go unreported. Weather forecast probabilities ("A 70-percent probability of snow tomorrow") are even less reliable because the "experience" consists of a great many separate factors, and an error in any one of them or in the way in which they are combined can wreck the entire calculation. Nevertheless, if the weather forecast calls for an 80-percent chance of snow, you'd be wise to bundle up.

The least reliable probability estimates are those in which the "experience" is not clearly defined and is gathered from individuals who may not be representative of the entire population. In a recent *New York Times* feature story on children who get mugged on their way to or from school, a member of New York's Safety and Fitness Exchange estimated that "before age 16, 25 to 50 percent of children will be accosted in some way." Aside from the fact that we don't know what "accosted in some way" means, we have no idea of the number of children on which the estimate was based, where they lived, or anything else about them. This kind of estimate, which is usually intended to create a sensation, need never be taken seriously.

Are They Up to Date?

Because the national census takes place only once every ten years, and because publication of the information takes time, some probability figures are likely to be several years out of date—although some are updated regularly. Figures on life expectancy don't change dramatically during the course of a few years, but figures on average family income often do. No matter what figures you look at, be sure to look also at the date when they were collected.

How Similar Are You to the Group on Which the Probability Is Based?

Suppose that X University accepts only 25 percent of students who apply for admission, and suppose that you now stand in the top tenth of your high-school class and have SAT scores in the top fifth of all students who took the SAT. Can you feel confident about being admitted? Only if your high-school class and all SAT takers are very similar to the group applying to X University. In fact, of course, your entire high-school class is very probably *not* like the applicants to X University, and the entire population of SAT takers is almost certainly not. In fact, you may very well find that *all* applicants to X University—and not just the 25 percent of them who get admitted—have class standings and SAT scores much like yours. If so, you have a 1-in-4 chance of being admitted. On the other hand, if you have perfect 800 SAT scores and a Westinghouse Talent Search Scholarship, you can be reasonably sure that not every other applicant is like you.

Similarly, if you read that about 10 percent of males have some sort of police record before they reach age twenty, should you assume that you, too, have a 1-in-10 chance of being arrested? Not necessarily, because the police don't arrest young people randomly. Arrests are far more common among poor, uneducated youth in the slums than in suburban neighborhoods. So your chances, if you're not a slum dweller, are substantially lower than 1 in 10.

On the other hand, don't assume in the absence of good evidence that you *are* different from the population on which the probability is based. If, for example, you read that only 50 percent of all applicants to medical schools get admitted, or that only 25 percent of college graduates get jobs that are related to their college majors, don't become overconfident simply because you say to yourself, "Well, I'm more motivated," "I'm smarter," or "I have a better personality." Unless you have good evidence—which is almost impossible to get on these characteristics—this kind of thinking is no more effective than whistling in the dark.

Do the Probabilities Frighten You More Than They Should?

Does the current emphasis on smoking as a cause of cancer make you overlook the fact that lung cancer is *not* the leading cause of death—and that you, like everyone else, will eventually die of *some* cause? This is not to suggest that you take up smoking; it suggests only that probabilities should not frighten you unduly. Reliable statistics show that male teenagers have a very much higher probability of being killed in automobile accidents than their elders, but the fact is that an overwhelming majority of teenagers *don't* die in car crashes—even though many of them have fender-bending accidents due to inexperience. Understanding this should not make you drive thoughtlessly, but it should prevent your parents from plunging into panic every time they lend you the keys to the family car.

9

Three out of Four Dentists . . .

"According to a recent survey . . ."

When you hear or read that three out of four dentists recommend Choo-Goo bubble gum, or that 47 percent of the voters disagree with the president's economic program, or that your favorite television program is going off the air because of poor ratings, the source of your information is some kind of poll or opinion survey that asked and collected the opinions of dentists, voters, or television viewers.

Whatever its purpose, a survey makes good scientific sense, because it replaces guesswork or speculation about what people think or what they plan to do with some kind of actual measurement of their opinions, preferences, or behavior. Indeed, it is precisely because surveys seem "scientific" that advertisers and politicians use them to persuade the public that a certain product or a political platform is "the people's choice." But, as we shall see, although good surveys are indeed "scientific," accurate, and useful, probably most surveys are none of the above.

Surveys can be done in several ways. Some use interviewers who ask people a series of questions, either face to face or by telephone; some use mail questionnaires. And some surveys, instead of asking questions, observe or measure people's actual behavior, often without their being aware that they are participating in a survey.

For example, the "Pepsi Challenge," instead of asking, "Do

you prefer Pepsi or Coke?" invited people to taste two un-
marked glasses of a cola drink and to report which of them
tasted better. Its conclusion was that most people preferred
Pepsi to Coke. (This is hardly surprising, because had the
results shown a preference for Coke, the survey certainly
would not have been featured on hundreds of Pepsi television
commercials.)

The Nielsen rating, which measures the popularity of television programs, connects to the TV sets of a group of supposedly typical listeners a device that records the length of
time the set is turned on and the channels to which it's tuned.
And many large manufacturing companies, before launching
a new product with a national advertising campaign, "test-
market" it to see how it fares on the supermarket shelves in a
few cities they regard as typical. In this kind of survey, the
shoppers in the test market are completely unaware that they
are serving as guinea pigs.

Obviously, the findings of such surveys range from the
trivial to the very important. The fact that people prefer
Pepsi to Coke, for example, is no reason for you to change
your own preference. But survey reports in the midst of a
political campaign can be very important. If, early in the
campaign, they report that candidate A has a substantial
lead, they may discourage the supporters of candidates B and
C and thus ensure their defeat. And surveys finding that 44
percent of the voters are displeased with the president's
handling of the economy may signal trouble not only for the
president but for the country as a whole, because it indicates
that the voters are very sharply divided.

QUESTIONING THE QUESTIONERS

But whether the topic is important or trivial, the basic question we need to answer is whether survey results are trustworthy—that is, whether we ought to *believe* every announcement that begins with the words, "According to a recent survey. . . ." Unfortunately, there is no simple, yes-or-no answer to this question, because the people who design and carry out surveys vary widely in their competence and their motives. But we can make a roughly accurate evaluation of any specific survey by subjecting it to some questions of our own.

Did People Tell Interviewers the Truth?

Perhaps the first question you have about surveys is "How do we know that people tell interviewers the truth?" or "What happens when they don't know the answer?" or "Why don't they tell interviewers to mind their own business?" When you consider the very personal questions that some survey interviewers ask—about income, for example, or sexual behavior, or family relationships—you would certainly suspect that many people would be embarrassed to tell the truth and would either give the interviewer an answer that would make them look good or would simply slam the door in her face.

There are, of course, certain survey questions that are more likely than others to produce untruthful answers. Students, for example, when speaking to interviewers, often exaggerate their grade-point averages. (We know this because their exaggeration shows up when the grades they report to interviewers are checked against their school records.) And most researchers suspect that many workers exaggerate their level of job satisfaction because they're ashamed to admit that they remain in a job that they don't like. In general, people seem most likely to exaggerate or distort their answers in the hope of making themselves more acceptable to the interviewer (who, of course, doesn't care one way or the other). This is why some students exaggerate their grade points—and why many adults don't admit to watching as much television as they actually do.

It's important, too, to bear in mind that most surveys study people's opinions and attitudes, not their actual behavior. And so, for example, although in a recent *New York Times* poll 30 percent of men said that they ought to help their wives more around the house, their actual behavior may not match their opinions. One respondent, according to the *New York Times*

> said when interviewed for the poll that he felt men should do half or more of the cooking; cleaning, and child caring. Asked if he should do more around his own home, he answered, "Yes, everything."
>
> But in a follow-up interview, he conceded, "I feel the ambition is there, but doing what I intend to do is a whole different story. I still get upset sometimes if my wife asks me to make the bed."

And the authors of *American Couples* conclude that even if a husband is unemployed he does much less housework than a wife who puts in a 40-hour week.

But the fact is that if the interviewer has been carefully selected and trained, he (or, more often, she, because most interviewers are women) is likely to get the truth most of the time from most of the people interviewed. There are several reasons for this. First, most people seem rather eager to talk about themselves to a sympathetic listener (and this is what an interviewer is trained to be). But when their opinions or actions are "odd" or "not very nice," they hesitate to confide them even to their best friends. An interviewer, on the other hand, is a stranger who doesn't know them personally and whom they are unlikely to meet ever again, and so they are more likely to tell the truth, even when it's somewhat embarrassing.

Furthermore, interviewers are trained to detect liars, not by looking them straight in the eye but by asking certain kinds of questions—called *validity checks*—the answers to which will match the answers to earlier questions if the person is telling the truth. An inconsistent answer to a validity check tells the interviewer that the person is lying and that his answers should not be taken seriously. Here's an example:

INTERVIEWER: "Do you do much reading?"
RESPONDENT: "Oh, yes! I use the town library all the time."
INTERVIEWER: "Can you tell me the name of a book you've read lately?"
RESPONDENT: "Well, uh . . ."

There is one fairly convincing proof that most people tell competent interviewers the truth: when high-quality surveys make a prediction—about the outcome of an election, for example—the prediction turns out to be right (or very close to right) most of the time. This could not happen unless the people interviewed were telling the truth—or unless each response was chosen by an equal proportion of liars, who thus cancel each other out.

In general, lying is not a serious problem, but ignorance is —because many people don't like to admit to an interviewer that they know nothing about an issue. If, for example, an interviewer asks your opinion on the issue of merit pay for teachers and you know nothing whatever about it, you might answer the question on the basis of your feelings about your favorite teacher rather than admit your ignorance. If you are asked whether you prefer American or foreign cars and you've had no experience with either, you might answer the question just to be polite, but your answer wouldn't be worth very much. Properly constructed interviews allow for an "I don't know" or a "No opinion" answer, and good interviewers are trained to make people feel comfortable about choosing it, but many people are ashamed to choose it. And so, if Mr. A and Mr. B are interviewed about a political issue, their answers will count equally, even if Mr. A has thought carefully about the issue and Mr. B knows nothing at all about it.

A person who is ashamed to tell the truth or to confess ignorance may, of course, simply refuse to be interviewed, and if a large number of people do this, the survey results will be distorted. When, for example, you read the results of a survey of the sexual behavior of high-school students, you are right in wondering whether they describe the behavior of high-school students in general or only of those who were willing to talk truthfully to the interviewers. The problem is, of course, that the sexual behavior of students who refused to cooperate may be widely different from the behavior of those who were willing to talk about it. But highly skilled interviewers are trained to persuade "refusers" to cooperate, and as a result this is not a major problem in surveys that are done carefully.

How Fair Were the Questions?

Although relatively few people lie to interviewers, their answers will produce inaccurate results if the questions are not worded properly. One type of improper wording produces a "loaded" or "leading" question—that is, a question that encourages one answer rather than another or that forces a response that may be inaccurate. The best-known example of a loaded question is "Have you stopped beating your wife?"—a question that many people cannot answer accurately with either a yes or a no. But the loaded questions that appear in survey interviews are usually less obvious. If, for example, an interviewer asks you, "Do you favor government regulation that stifles initiative and increases the cost of doing business?" does your "no" answer mean that you are opposed to *all* government regulation? The chances are that this is how your answer will be interpreted.

Would you answer both of the following questions with a yes or a no?

1. Do you think that the cream of American manhood should be sent overseas to fight to preserve a corrupt democracy?
2. Do you think that the United States should lend its military support to a small democracy whose existence is threatened by a powerful totalitarian country?

These questions were asked, a few years ago, by researchers interested in testing the effects of loaded questions. Not surprisingly, the first question got an overwhelmingly negative response from the very same people who gave the second question an overwhelmingly positive response. Both questions referred, of course, to the Vietnam War—and both were equally loaded.

Some questions, such as the one on government regulation, which was taken from a newsletter published by a Republican congressman, are loaded in a deliberate attempt to influence the responses. But often loaded questions are the result of thoughtlessness. When asked, for example, "Which is your favorite airline?" some people will express a preference rather than admit that they've never flown.

Survey results will be inaccurate also if the questions don't cover a range broad enough to provide for all possible answers. If, for example, you are asked only whether you would prefer candidate A or candidate B to be elected, but you actually prefer candidate C, is your answer likely to predict your actual vote?

One way to evaluate a survey, then, is to scrutinize the questions. Good professional surveys always provide, along with the results, the actual questions that were asked, and responsible newspapers usually include them in their reports. But if the questions are not available, you are right to suspect that they may have been loaded. Were the three out of four dentists who recommended Choo-Goo bubble gum asked, "Which brand of gum do you recommend to your patients?" or "Which brand of *bubble* gum do you recommend to your patients *who chew gum?*"

There are other ways in which incompetent or deliberately dishonest surveys can influence their results in advance. Not long ago, a wine company offered customers a cash rebate if they bought a bottle of the company's wine and checked on the rebate coupon their response to one of the following questions: "Yes, I agree Taylor California Cellars light wines are delicious"; or "Sorry, I am not satisfied." Customers who checked the first answer were promised a $1.50 rebate, but customers who checked the second would get only $1. Yet, if the results are published, readers are hardly likely to learn about this bias.

Who Got Left Out?

If you would like to do a survey of your classmates' opinions about the new algebra teacher, it would not be difficult for you to interview all twenty or thirty students—that is, 100 percent of the "population" whose opinion you want to measure. But a survey that attempts to measure the political opinions of the American voter or the brand preferences of the American housewife can't possibly interview 100 percent of the millions of voters or housewives. And so the people planning the survey select for their interviews a *sample* of the population in which they're interested.

Sampling may strike you as fairly easy. After all, if you want to "sample" a bag of peppermints to see what they taste like, you pick any piece at random, because you're sure that it will taste like every other piece. But people, obviously, are not as similar as pieces of candy, and so, if a survey is to measure national opinion, the sample it uses must be representative of the population as a whole—in income, in education, and in its proportion of males to females, or Democrats to Republicans, or city people to country people.

A mistake in sampling can make survey results worthless. About fifty years ago a national news magazine, in an early attempt at opinion polling, surveyed ten million people (a sample of record size) all over the country on their voting intentions in the upcoming presidential election. On the basis of the responses, the editors confidently predicted a Republican victory—but the Democrats won in a landslide.

What had gone wrong? The poll had been done honestly, but the pollsters' mailing lists came largely from telephone directories, and in those days only the well-to-do had telephones. And the well-to-do, then as now, tended to vote Republican. The survey had failed to sample the millions of people who could not afford telephones and who, as usual, voted for the Democratic ticket. Shortly afterwards the magazine, having lost its credibility, went out of business.

Since those early days, pollsters have become much more sophisticated, and computers have simplified the complicated and laborious statistical techniques used to select a representative sample. And now that most people have telephones, polls using telephone interviews are less inaccurate than they once were—provided they take care to include people who have unlisted numbers. But many polls still use unrepresentative samples, sometimes because the people conducting them lack the money or the skill needed to obtain a representative sample, but often because a biased sample—that is, a sample that omits some kinds of people—is more likely to give them the results they would like to get.

In general, the bigger the sample, the more likely it is to be representative. Obviously the college freshman who, on his first walk through campus, saw a staggering-drunk student supported by two sober friends and reported to his parents that one-third of the students were drunks was using too small a sample. But through the use of the right statistical techniques a sample can be quite small and yet representative. The *New York Times*/CBS poll, for example, which has proved accurate time after time, uses only about 1,450 people as a representative sample of the entire U.S. population. (Perhaps this is why most people complain that they have never been interviewed.)

The smaller the sample used, the greater the likelihood that the results will be inaccurate, but pollsters, by the use of statistics, can measure the amount of this error quite accurately. The *New York Times*/CBS poll's sample of 1,450 produces a margin of error of about 4 percent, and this is why, when voter preferences for two candidates differ by only 4 or 5 percent, the pollsters made no prediction and say merely that the election is "too close to call." Using a larger sample would, of course, reduce this margin of error but would cost too much in both money and time.

Usually, however, errors occur not because the sample was too small but because it omitted groups of people whose responses would alter the results. This is especially true of mail questionnaires—which are almost always untrustworthy. When a questionnaire is sent by mail, it is usually filled out and returned by only 5 percent of the people who receive it— that is, only one out of twenty. The small size of this response is not the problem. (After all, the 1,450-person sample used to represent the entire U.S. population is far smaller than 5 percent). But the 5 percent of people who respond to mail questionnaires are likely *not* to be representative of the population being surveyed.

To begin with, they are people who are very conscientious about answering their mail, and such people are likely to differ in many ways from those who treat mail from strangers more casually. Then, too, they are likely to be people whose feelings about the issue are far stronger than the 95 percent of recipients who throw the questionnaire into the nearest wastebasket.

Let's look, for example, at a questionnaire about automobile insurance that Consumers Union published not long ago in an issue of its magazine *Consumer Reports*. To begin with, because the questionnaire was printed as part of the magazine, filling it out would require a reader to cut the page out—something that many readers hesitate to do with a magazine that they file for future reference. The reader would also have to take the time and trouble to find and address an envelope and mail it at his own expense.

Obviously, the questionnaire was more likely to be answered by readers who were furiously angry with their insurance companies (and possibly by readers who were passionately happy with them) than by automobile owners who were moderately satisfied or moderately dissatisfied but not enough so to go to the trouble of returning the questionnaire. But Consumers Union could never know whether this was

The New York Times/CBS NEWS POLL
Attitudes on the Economy

"Some people say the recession is over and think an economic recovery has begun. Do you think that's true or not?"

Percentage of respondents who . . .

. . . believe recession is over	. . . do not believe recession is over

TOTAL SAMPLE
42% 53%

INCOME
$40,000 and over: 62 31
$20,000-40,000: 48 50
Under $20,000: 34 61

REGION
East: 39 56
Midwest: 42 53
South: 41 54
West: 49 47

RACE
Whites: 46 49
Blacks: 17 81

Poll of 1,489 adults conducted April 7-11, 1983. Those with no opinion are not shown.

Method
Used in Poll

The latest New York Times/ CBS News Poll is based on telephone interviews conducted from April 7 through 11 with 1,489 adults around the United States, excluding Alaska and Hawaii.

The telephone exchanges called were selected by a computer from a complete list of exchanges in the country. They were chosen in a way to insure that each region was represented in proportion to its population. The telephone numbers were formed by random digits, thus permitting access to both listed and unlisted numbers.

The results have been weighted to take account of household size and variations in the sample relating to region, race, sex, age and education.

In theory, it can be said that 19 times out of 20 the results based on the entire sample differ by no more than three percentage points in either direction from what would have been obtained by interviewing all adult Americans. The error for smaller subgroups is larger. For instance, the margin of sampling error for persons with family incomes over $40,000 is plus or minus eight percentage points, and for those under $20,000 it is four percentage points either way.

Besides sampling error, the practical difficulties of conducting any survey of public opinion may introduce other sources of error into the poll.

Assisting The Times in its 1983 survey coverage is Dr. Irving Crespi of Irving Crespi and Associates, a survey consulting firm.

Opinion polls are interesting not merely for their overall findings but for the differences between the opinions of various groups of respondents. As we might expect, the well-to-do are far more optimistic about the economy than those with below-average incomes; blacks are especially pessimistic because a disproportionate percentage of them are poor. Which group has the smallest number of "No opinion" responses, and why do you think this is so? Is the question phrased in neutral terms? Because respondents are more likely to agree with the question than disagree with it, some experts would argue that these results may be biased because the question is posed in a positive rather than a negative form; their approach might be to phrase the question positively to half the sample and negatively to the other half.

The box on this page, which appears each time the New York Times/CBS News Poll is published, not only describes the sample and the method but also helps readers understand the limitations of the poll's accuracy.

true or not—or whether the responses accurately represented the feelings of most of its readers. In addition, because the readers of *Consumer Reports* tend to be in the top 10 percent of the U.S. population in terms of income and education, they can certainly not be a representative sample of all automobile owners.

Consumers Union did not introduce these biases deliberately in order to influence the results. It used a mail questionnaire (which almost *always* produces a biased sample) because obtaining a representative one would have been far too costly. It would involve selecting and interviewing a group of automobile owners of both sexes and a wide range of ages who drive all kinds of cars in all parts of the country.

Now that a television set has become a standard household appliance, television is being used for two kinds of "instant polling." In the first type, viewers are asked, after watching the president discuss a problem, or after a debate on some controversial issue, to register their opinions by calling a telephone number displayed on the screen. Obviously, the respondents are an unrepresentative sample for two reasons. First, only people who watch the program are likely to respond. And, second, since the phone call usually costs the viewer 50 cents, the poll is likely to exclude anyone who can't afford the call or doesn't think it's worth the price. For these reasons such poll results are likely to favor the conservative rather than the liberal side of an issue—which is exactly what occurred in the ill-fated news magazine poll we mentioned a few pages back. Unfortunately, when the results of such a poll are announced, there is likely to be no mention of these biases.

A second type of television polling, now available on an experimental basis to cable subscribers in three or four test cities, permits the viewer to transmit his opinion on an issue to the studio simply by pressing a control button on his set. This kind of polling is even more biased, since it is limited to cable subscribers as well as to those who happened to be watching and were interested enough to register their responses.

Sometimes, of course, pollsters may deliberately bias a sample in order to produce the responses they would like to see. Not long ago, for example, the Republican National Committee mailed out a questionnaire that told the recipients that their responses would not be counted unless they were accompanied by a campaign contribution. Now, if this survey was interested only in the opinions of people willing to contribute money to the Republican party, there was nothing wrong with this method of choosing a sample. But if the results were published with the statement that they repre- sented "public opinion," or even the opinions of "Republican voters," then the sample would be highly unrepresentative.

Not every sample, of course, needs to be representative of the entire U.S. population. The "Pepsi Challenge," for exam- ple, used passersby who stopped at the survey booths out of curiosity and who apparently drank cola often enough to be interested in participating in a survey that offered them a free taste in return for a minute or two of their time. This sample would be representative of cola drinkers as long as it was reasonably large and included people from several parts of the country, because soft-drink preferences vary by region. Given the purpose of the survey, there was no reason to in- clude people who never touch soft drinks.

In general, high-quality surveys always include as part of their report a description of the survey sample (although your local newspaper may not include this detail when it reports the results). Advertising agencies, on the other hand, and other survey organizations that do surveys for manufacturers of toothpaste or for politicians almost never describe their sample. After all, the pollsters who claim that "Three out of four dentists recommend Choo-Goo gum" may, if they were very lucky, have used a sample of only four dentists and quit while they were ahead.

What Else Is Going on?

On many issues public opinion changes rapidly—sometimes overnight. It can be changed by military or political events— as it was by the hostage situation in Iran or by the U.S. invasion of Grenada—or by rapid changes in the economy. In fact, one of the major uses of opinion surveys is to measure week-to-week changes in the voters' opinions of presidential candidates during an election year.

To understand the significance of any survey results, you need to note, first, the dates on which the opinions were recorded. If the results are more than a couple of months old, they may be outdated. But even if the survey was conducted very recently—no more than a week ago—you need to consider whether it reflects fairly stable opinions or opinions that are influenced by some crisis or other unusual event.

PUTTING IT ALL TOGETHER

As we've seen, there is no need for you to accept the results of an opinion survey on blind faith. Instead, you can try to evaluate the survey in terms of the elements we've been discussing. You can examine the questions to see whether they're likely to produce untruthful answers. You can scrutinize the wording of the questions for any evidence of loading, ambiguity, or restriction of choice. And you can ask yourself whether the sample was a representative one in terms of the purpose of the survey.

But some of these suggestions are easier to make than to carry out. Spotting badly worded questions can take a great deal of training and experience, because sometimes their defects are far from obvious. And deciding whether a sample is both representative and adequately large often requires a knowledge of statistics. Often, too, the information you need about question wording and about the composition of the sample simply isn't available—perhaps for good reason. But even with these limitations, you can make some reasonably accurate estimates about the trustworthiness of survey results by knowing something about the motivations of the organization that did the work and about the competence of the people involved.

The most highly professional survey organizations—the Gallup Poll, the National Opinion Research Corporation, the Harris Poll, and one or two others—can be trusted because they are independent. That is, they alone decide which topics to survey and how to survey them. They earn a living not by undertaking research for clients interested only in results that are favorable to them but by selling their findings to the news media and to any other organizations that would find them useful, no matter what their conclusions. This means that these survey organizations can be completely objective in their surveys because they have no personal interest in having the results come out one way rather than another. And it is this professional objectivity that enables them to attract the very best-trained people to design the questionnaires and to carry out the interviews.

But in terms of sheer numbers, far more surveys are done by survey firms who work under contract to advertising agencies, public-relations firms, or political candidates. These clients obviously expect that the surveys they pay for will show that most people favor their product or their platform, and so such surveys are always open to the suspicion that either the sample or the questions were somehow "doctored" to make the results favor the client. Of course, if the results *don't* come out favoring the client, you can be sure that they will never be published.

Often advertising agencies will not bother with the services of survey organizations and simply put together a television commercial that conveys a "man-in-the-street" feeling by showing a very unhandsome model with a "street" accent and an unglamorous name "blind-testing" two beers and expressing delighted surprise when he discovers that he has chosen the sponsor's beer. This kind of charade should not, of course, be confused with an opinion survey—not even a bad one. But, more important, even a properly conducted survey showing that people prefer Product A over Product B should not change your own tastes if you happen to prefer Product B. Of course, if low Nielsen ratings knock your favorite television program off the air, there's nothing you can do about it.

Surveys are sometimes done by complete amateurs—by club leaders who want to learn how members feel about the club's program, by teachers curious about how their students respond to them, by community groups interested in the opinions of an entire neighborhood on a proposed zoning change. Although the intentions of such people are usually good, the results are likely to be unreliable for reasons that you now understand—poorly phrased questions and improper sampling. In such surveys the defects are likely to be so obvious that, now that you know what to look for, you can separate the reliable ones from the faulty ones with a good deal of confidence.

10

Can We Ever Be Sure?

"Science is a bunch of rules that keep us from lying to each other."

—*an eminent biologist*

Although you've probably learned a good deal from the preceding chapters, it would not be surprising if you approached this last chapter feeling somewhat puzzled, troubled—maybe even annoyed. After all, you have discovered that some things you accepted as true are, in fact, false, and that some things you assumed were false are true —and this is never an entirely comfortable experience.

Perhaps one source of your puzzlement may be our repeated use of such phrases as "Scientists have discovered . . ." or "Research studies indicate . . ." or "The statistics show. . . ." Why, you may ask, do we put so much faith in scientists? Haven't scientists been proved wrong in the past? Don't honest scientists honestly disagree with one another and, indeed, aren't some scientists dishonest? And why do we put so much faith in statistics? Can't even reliable statistics be wrong? On the other hand, can't something be true even if it isn't backed by statistical evidence? And, perhaps most important, should we demand a "scientific" answer to every conceivable question? These questions are well worth asking, and they can best be answered by an explanation of how scientists work.

GUILTY UNTIL PROVEN INNOCENT

Although the American system of justice prides itself on the principle that persons accused of a crime are considered innocent until proven guilty, scientists work the opposite way. They assume that a theory is false unless it meets certain standards. This is why, for example, physicians don't use a new and untested cancer treatment on their patients with the notion, "Well, how do we know it *won't* work?" Instead, they insist on good evidence that it *does* work. Math teachers may be very eager to find a better way of teaching calculus, but they aren't going to adopt a new plan until they have good evidence that it works on students like those in their own classroom. This "good evidence" is developed in several steps, but it always begins with the scientist who originates the new treatment or the new teaching technique.

Is It Significant?

Let's suppose that an educational psychologist wants to discover whether only children or children with one brother or sister are more likely to earn doctoral degrees than children with three or more brothers and sisters. He might go about the research by comparing a sample of current doctoral candidates or recent doctoral graduates at several universities with a sample of unsuccessful applicants to doctoral programs and asking each of them the number of their brothers and sisters and their parents' income. After analyzing their responses, he might conclude that, when income is not a factor, children from small families are, indeed, more likely to earn doctoral degrees. Or he might reach the same conclusion after getting a sample of college students, dividing them into a small-family group and a large-family group, and questioning them about their educational plans.

But in either case, his findings are open to an important question: How do we know that his results aren't due to sheer chance—the chance that he just "happened" to find samples in which the children from small families were more likely to get doctoral degrees? To put the same question another way, how do we know that a different sample chosen from the same population might not give him very different results?

The answer is that we can *never* be absolutely certain that his (or any other) scientific findings are not due to chance. This always remains a possibility. But what we *can* do is to determine *how likely* it is that a set of scientific conclusions is due to sheer chance. The way this is done is by applying to the findings a "test of statistical significance."

Although the test itself involves very complex mathematical procedures, what it establishes can be explained quite simply: it tells us the probability that the findings are not real but merely resulted from chance. And so, although it can never tell us that the results are absolutely "true," it can show that there was only a 1-in-20 (that is, 5 percent) or a 1-in-100 (1 percent) probability that the findings resulted by chance.

As a group, scientists are highly self-critical, and if our scientist's test of significance shows that his findings had a more-than-5-percent probability of being due to mere chance, he may abandon the research on the grounds that his findings were "not significant" or he may redesign it in the hope of getting findings that test "below the 5-percent level." In any event, you are most unlikely ever to hear of any research findings that don't meet this test.

Publish or Perish
As you may have heard, every scientist, whatever her field, is required to "publish or perish." This means that if she ex-

pects a lifetime career in scientific work at a university or a research institution, she must regularly submit the results of her research for publication in a scientific journal. If she doesn't publish with reasonable frequency, she will "perish" because no university or research center will employ her.

The reason for this stress on publication is far more important than simply getting her name in print. It is, rather, the only way in which she can let her fellow scientists know what she is doing so that they can criticize her findings or apply them to their own work. And you may be certain that if her work contains flaws or errors, her colleagues will be quick to point them out—again in articles that will be published in the scientific journals.

But even before publication, her research will be subjected to critical scrutiny. Unlike the editors of popular magazines, who rely on their own hunches in choosing materials that will interest their readers, the editors of scientific journals submit every contribution to a group of advisory experts, who "referee" it to make certain that it meets scientific standards —not only in terms of statistical significance (which usually must be at the 1- or 2-percent level) but in terms of the significance of its conclusions. These standards are so strict that the most highly respected scientific journals reject more than 80 percent of the manuscripts submitted to them. In general, then, when you read something in a scientific journal —or an accurate media summary of something that has appeared in a scientific journal—you can trust it. In fact, no reputable scientist will offer his findings to the mass media— and no responsible editor would take them seriously—until they had been published in a scientific journal.

But this process of critical review raises another question: If the advisory boards of the scientific journals consist of recognized "establishment" authorities, what chance of publication does a young scientist have if his research challenges their views? Isn't it likely that these authorities will simply reject his contribution as "unsound"? Didn't Galileo have to retract his theory (even though it proved to be correct) because it contradicted the views of the establishment?

This question can't be answered in one word, but the answer is more likely to be no than yes. We must bear in mind that scientists, unlike the Catholic Church of Galileo's day, make decisions not on the basis of belief but on the basis of scientific evidence. And if they are confronted with convincing evidence, they are likely to accept it even if it runs contrary to what they currently believe to be "true."

In general, the notion that new knowledge is created by scientific underdogs who face the opposition of the entire scientific establishment is simply not true. Isaac Newton's scientific contributions changed the face of science, but Newton was in no way a "rebel." He was a highly respected member of the scientific community long before he made his major contribution. And, despite what you may have learned in your history class, Columbus was certainly not the first man to suggest that the earth was round. Almost every scientist of his day thought so.

ARE ALL SCIENTISTS HONEST?

Although there appears to be no research on the subject, it seems likely that scientists are neither more nor less honest than other people but, like all of us, they may become dishonest in some circumstances. Under pressure to publish or perish, or in an attempt to prove a preconceived notion, some scientists have fabricated results instead of discovering them in the laboratory, and some have changed their findings to bring them into better agreement with their hypotheses.

This kind of work has, every once in a while, escaped detection by the reviewers, but sooner or later these scientists get caught—either by some keen-eyed colleague who finds flaws in their results or by other scientists who repeat the original experiment but find that they don't get the same results.

Sometimes, of course, this detection comes later rather than sooner. The British psychologist Cyril Burt achieved worldwide fame for his thirty-year study of twins that "proved" that intelligence was inherited rather than acquired from the environment. In fact, for several decades Burt's work was so widely accepted that younger scientists used it as a starting point for their own research. It was not until the 1970s, when the issue of intelligence again attracted a great deal of attention, that a young psychologist reviewing some of Burt's later work became suspicious of some of Burt's figures, decided that they looked "too good to be true," recalculated them, and found that Burt had almost certainly faked them in order to support his theory and that Burt's work was without any scientific value. But the Burt case is quite unusual, and it should not make us broadly suspicious of scientists as a group. And, oddly enough, whether or not Burt faked his data, similar work by other scientists supported Burt's conclusions.

UNANTICIPATED CONSEQUENCES

Sometimes a scientific finding turns out to be "wrong" not because the scientist was careless or dishonest but because he could not see the whole picture. A few decades ago, for example, pediatricians who dealt with premature infants recognized that many of them died through lack of oxygen because their lungs were not sufficiently developed to use the oxygen from the air around them. And so, by introducing a flow of pure oxygen into the hospital incubator, they were able to reduce the death rate dramatically.

It was not until several years had passed that the pediatricians began noticing that these oxygen-supplemented infants had a high frequency of blindness, and still more time passed before it was recognized that the blindness—a condition called *retrolental fibroplasia*—was caused by the high concentration of oxygen. Today the oxygen concentration in incubators has been reduced, but until its effects were discovered, the use of a high concentration of oxygen for premature newborns was regarded as a "good" scientific discovery.

Because, like retrolental fibroplasia, many of the consequences of science or technology don't show up immediately, it's important to recognize that many new discoveries —no matter how cautiously and conscientiously developed —simply can't be evaluated immediately. And this is one reason why the U.S. Food and Drug Administration often takes a very long time before approving a new drug as safe and effective, and even FDA approval occasionally turns out to have been a mistake. As one scientist has put it, "Let us not follow truth too closely from behind lest we get kicked in the teeth."

ARE YOU UP TO DATE?

On the other hand, following the truth too closely may be less hazardous and a good deal less common than being behind the times. By the time a scientific theory or discovery makes its way through the media, into the textbooks, and ultimately into the minds of large numbers of people, it may well be out of date. As John Kenneth Galbraith, the Harvard economist, has pointed out, by the time everybody "knows" something, it is probably no longer true.

This holds true not only today, when new knowledge is being created more rapidly than ever before, but also for ideas that have been around for a long time. Adam Smith, the British economist, published his theory of a competitive market governed by the laws of supply and demand more than 200 years ago. Even in his own day, Smith's theoretical model was far from perfect, and today it is dangerously deficient in explaining the economy of the United States. Yet the economic thinking of a great many people remains based entirely on Adam Smith's theory.

WHAT SCIENCE IS—AND WHAT IT ISN'T

When President Franklin D. Roosevelt faced the economic crisis of the 1930s, he called in a famous economist and asked, "Should the United States go off the gold standard?" The economist replied, "Mr. President, I can tell you what will probably happen if it *does*, and I can tell you what will probably happen if it *doesn't*. But whether it *should* or not is for you to decide, not for me."

This fifty-year-old anecdote illustrates a very important limitation of science—a limitation more likely to be recognized by the scientists themselves than by people in general. Scientists legitimately use "is" or "will be" to describe or to predict phenomena; but "should" or "ought" applies to values, not to facts, and in this area scientists have no more authority than any other citizen. Thus, a nuclear physicist or a biochemist invited by a congressional committee to serve as an "expert witness" may be especially qualified, because of his professional knowledge, to describe to the committee the probable effects of a nuclear bomb on civilian populations. But if he joins a "Ban the Bomb" movement, he is acting as a private citizen on the basis of his personal values—even though he may be more informed than others. When scientists express their personal values—by joining organizations or by writing letters to the editors of newspapers—you may want to pay close attention to their technical arguments, but with respect to their viewpoints about what *should* be done you should bear in mind that they are acting as private citizens and deserve no more and no less respect than other private citizens.

Science has another limitation that often frustrates nonscientists: it can deal only with what is observable and measurable. And, although technological advances such as the cyclotron, the electron microscope, the radio telescope, and the CAT scanner make more and more of the world observable and measurable, some phenomena will clearly remain unobservable, unmeasurable, or both. This is why science can't provide the answers to many very interesting questions: whether ghosts exist, whether there is life after death, whether a communist society is better or worse than our own, or whether you are likely to be "happy" with your marriage or your career.

WHERE DO WE STAND NOW?

Once you understand its limitations, you are likely to develop a rather high degree of respect for the scientific approach. But there is a danger that you may overestimate its achievements and feel that today we know almost everything there is to be known. Having learned the periodic table in your first-year chemistry class, you may, for example, look down on the Greek philosopher Empedocles, who, in the fifth century B.C., announced that all matter was made up of four elements—air, water, earth, and fire. Or you may think that Ptolemy and the other early astronomers were "pretty dumb" to believe that the earth was the center of the universe.

Trained scientists don't take this condescending view. They recognize that their own work has depended almost entirely on the work (and the errors) of scientists who preceded them and who were every bit as intelligent but who lacked the sophisticated instruments and the accumulated knowledge that today's scientists enjoy. As Isaac Newton expressed it, "If I have seen further, it is by standing on ye shoulders of giants."

Once you understand that our knowledge is based on probability rather than certainty—that each step is a closer approach to truth but not necessarily *the* truth—you may be ready to concede that a century from now your great-great-grandchildren may look back on the world you live in today with the same mixture of pity and condescension that you may be feeling about the Middle Ages.

Index